Copyright © 2023 by Philip Smith

TABLE OF CONTENTS

Leadership Toolbox

By

Philip Smith

Author's Dedication

To my children who inspire me every day to reach farther and my wife who gives me the support to reach my fullest potential.

INTRODUCTION

Every leader needs to have a toolbox full of tools to be successful. Just like the craftsman needs tools of the trade to get the job done, the leader needs to have a toolbox that enables leadership of a team. We often see that different tools can be used for similar jobs. Some tools are more fitting in one circumstance than others, but sometimes can be harmlessly interchangeable. In leadership, the tools that you have in your toolbox will shape the way that people around you react to your leadership style.

Leading people is either the highlight of a career or the lowest moment of that career. The way that we perceive leadership revolves around how prepared we are for the position. The tools that we have in our toolbox directly impacts the way that we feel about the position that we hold. Leaders who are prepared with the right tools or those who easily adapt the tools that they have are more likely to enjoy leadership than those who are unprepared.

The good news is, you can get new tools and begin enjoying leadership at any point in your career. For the cost of a good screwdriver, you can pick up a leadership book that gives you insights to develop tools that guide you throughout your career.

We are often shaped by the leaders that we have worked for. We use the same tools that we watched our leaders use. When we are not exposed to innovations in the tools that are available, we don't know that we can go out and pick up a better tool.

Could you imagine using only a handsaw because your boss was too cheap to let you know there are miter saws on the market? It would not be fun.

We use the tools that we know are out there.

There are absent leaders, toxic leaders, and bitter leaders that often have the opportunity to develop the next generation of leaders. My goal with this book is to help new leaders develop a toolbox they can pull from to effectively lead and manage their teams.

Leadership has the ability to multiply what individuals put into an organization. A good leader leverages the effort of a team to create more results than any single individual in a team can create. As leaders, we are responsible for the output of our teams. Our ability to guide and motivate our teams directly correlates to the success or failure we bring to our organization.

Effective leaders enable their team to work and clear the obstacles that slow the team down. Some team members will need training and guidance. Not all team members will be able to perform right out of the gate. Some team members will have high-performing periods followed by lower-performing periods. As leaders, we get to help people unlock and reach their potential. Leading requires a different set of tools compared to what we use to perform. How do we gain the tools we need? Experience and education will help us gain tools that will work for us.

So how did my journey with leadership develop my perspective?

When I was a young child, I took karate with my dad. Later, my sister and eventually my mom joined the school with us. During my time at the karate school, my dad began teaching classes at the school. He often had my family assist in the classes he was teaching. We would participate as demonstrators, practice partners, and as assistants to the other students. We would show up early and leave late. We were teaching at a remote branch of the school, and our family would dedicate our time to ensuring that the studio was ready for the students to show up and jump into lessons. During that time, I watched my dad build relationships with the students that he was responsible

2

for teaching. He dedicated himself to getting to know the students and providing a connection for them in more than karate training alone. He established himself as someone the students could rely on and trust. I was learning about servant leadership firsthand. My dad was giving himself to the people he was teaching. He wanted to clear every obstacle that might present for the students in his class.

By the time I got to high school, we had parted ways with the karate school we attended. I found wrestling as a sport and spent all four years of high school in wrestling. I was never a great wrestler. I don't think I had a season where I ever won much more than half of my matches. I was passionate about it, though. My coach recognized it and made me one of our team captains my junior and senior year. Passion for the team and passion for the sport were more important in a leadership role than the best wrestler on the team. The best wrestler in my two years as captain was a freshman and then sophomore who went undefeated until the last match of his sophomore year. He was not prepared to motivate anyone, though. He was too focused on his performance. He was not concerned about the team performance. Team captain was an interesting leadership role, especially on a wrestling team. In wrestling, everyone contributes individually to the team's success. As team captains, we motivated the team, we warmed the team up for practice, and we supported the team in getting prep-work done. We always had the support of the coaches as team captains. It was a leadership role that offered support in learning. My coach said something every year that helped shape my view of a leader. Every day we mopped the mats before practice. Coach would often grab a mop and mop with us. He said, "when I'm too important to mop, I need to retire." Coach did not want any of us to let our egos get ahead of us supporting the team. When we are too good to support our teams, we need to leave. There is no one on the team who has more of a right than anyone else on the team. As leaders, we need to check our egos.

3

In college, I was in Army ROTC. ROTC is a leadership development program. There is a great story that I will save for our chapter on coaching that led me to ROTC, but it was an example of brief leadership that shaped the course of my life. Throughout college, I had a cadre of leaders that dedicated themselves to teaching, guiding, mentoring, shaping, and evaluating the cadets within the program. The dedication of the cadre was beyond question. The cadre were our advocates. They looked for reasons to help us succeed, but they provided honest feedback. We were there to learn and grow. Without honesty in evaluations, we would leave thinking we had succeeded when there was room for growth. I feel fortunate to have succeeded in the program. There were cadets who self-selected out of the program and left because it was not for them. There were cadets who were weeded out because they screwed up. There were cadets who were dismissed because they could not meet standards. I screwed up while I was in the program. Being a young college kid, I was having too much fun and allowed myself to get in trouble while partying. It could have gone a few different ways, but the cadre, especially the commander, decided I was worth saving. I was shown grace from the leadership. I was punished. I lost part of my scholarship. I had to tell my whole unit what I had done. I spent the better part of a year reminding them not to make similar mistakes. I had been shown grace, though. I was allowed to stay in the program, graduate, and become an officer in the Army.

My experience with leadership through college was always a positive interaction with leadership. I know that I saw and worked with bad leaders, but the impact on me was minimal. I worked construction during college and had a foreman who didn't put safety first. I had an accident that could have been life-changing as a result, but it made its way into the footnotes of my story. Not the theme. I had peer leaders in ROTC that were arrogant, but they did not leave a lasting impression. I was fortunate to leave college with a positive view of leaders.

When I began my Army career, I learned about leaders that were not as positive as the experience that I had to date. I also had to experience the effects of my leadership in practice for the first time. While I knew about leadership and had some practice, I still had to develop my leadership style. At 22 years old, I had a platoon of 37 Soldiers that I was responsible for. I was also one of the newest people in my unit. I had seasoned leaders in my platoon that I was responsible for leading; it was a challenge.

In my Army career, I learned a lot about leadership in both direct and supporting roles. I led the 37 Soldier platoon for almost a year.

I spent 18 months working in a basic training unit making sure that the drill sergeants had the land, ammo, and resources that they needed to train civilians into Soldiers. I worked in a 3-Star Headquarters where I had to develop my authority through knowledge and trust because I was one of the lowest-ranking officers. The Army offered a lot of opportunities to learn about leadership. I was fortunate to command a company of Engineer Soldiers in the reserves after I left active duty while I was going through medical retirement. I had to modify the way I led to match my current conditions. I was not able to do the things I used to be able to do as a leader, but I had a great company, and we did great things.

In my civilian career, I began to understand that the toolbox that I had for leading is not the same as everyone else's. The Army has a strong leadership focus. The Army talks about leadership roles and development frequently. In the Army, everyone needs to understand leadership. Enlisted Soldiers become informal leaders early but are expected to be leaders when they reach Non-commissioned Officer. Officers are expected to perform in leadership roles as soon as they commission. When I transitioned to the civilian world, I found those conversations are not as frequent. People often get thrown into management and leadership roles without training or preparation. People who do well at their jobs are asked to lead other people. Performing and leading are different skill sets, but when we need leaders, we promote our best workers. For some, the career progression is great. For others, leadership is a miserable experience.

A friend of mine, Jay, in the civilian world made a huge impact on my passion for leadership development. I was a senior project manager for a utility construction company. Jay worked in the maintenance department of the same company. He had mentioned that he was not sure he was being fully utilized in his current role. He worked in the same office as his boss. He developed systems that increased the efficiency of the maintenance department company-wide. He felt that there was a lot of value he could offer, but that he did not feel that his ideas were heard. After discussing an opening that I was planning in the project management office, we moved him to my department. We spent the next year growing the position. I laid out my visions on where the role would grow to, and he offered ideas that could support the growth I envisioned or where he thought that I may be off in the vision with the goal of shaping the vision. We spent more than a year working together and shaping the role. The maintenance department wanted Jay back. The maintenance department had the capacity to offer him a raise and a promise of greater leadership within the organization. He took the position which benefited his family the most. The maintenance department got him.

Before he switched positions, Jay thanked me for my leadership style and told me that he hoped to emulate my leadership style in future positions. He had been raised in the construction industry by his father who was his foreman. His dad was an authoritarian leader. There was no questioning his dad's leadership. What was stated is what was expected. If you did not agree, you know how to get home. His boss in the shop offered a laissez-faire approach mixed with an authoritarian approach. He would often drop tasks on my buddy but would not look at the workload that was on his plate. He also did not expect to be questioned on the work that he assigned. There was little follow-up assigned tasks prior to due dates. My buddy couldn't question the tasks he was assigned, but he also didn't receive guidance or priorities. When Jay came to work for me, I did not lead as an expert. I wanted to leverage the talents of my team for greater success. Everyone on the team had access to me. Whether we were discussing our families, our goals, or work, we built trust. I worked to ensure that my team understood if I asked them to generate something, I was going to use it. Nothing was created solely for the sake of creation. I also worked to understand what I was asking and how it impacted on the team. Rarely did I ever get angry in front of my team. I was committed to developing relationships with the team that enhanced performance.

When my Jay told me that he was going to take my leadership style to his future roles, he was letting me know that I had added another tool or two to his toolbox. He did not have to lay down the law to get people to do what was needed. He could work with people and motivate them to do the work that he needed them to do. He did not say that he was going to throw out his old tools. He now had different ways to engage with people. He could take a gentle approach before taking a directive approach. He is also able to look at which tools best fit with which employee.

THE 5 W'S OF LEADERSHIP

Who?

What?

Where?

When?

Why?

You are probably reading this book because you are looking for ways to be more effective in leadership roles. Whether you are stepping into a leadership role for the first time, or you are an established leader, there is always room for growth. The best leaders stay the best because they are constantly learning, evolving, and developing their leadership. In order for us to develop our leadership style, it is important to know how to break leadership down into digestible components. I love using the 5 Ws we learned at the beginning of our scholastic career. Who? What? Where? When? Why? Without adding anything to each word, we are able to convey a full question. When we expand our questions, we can begin to see the shape of our environment.

A few years ago, I was working on a master's degree, and I had to conduct leadership interviews. I thought of a mentor that

I had when I was deployed to Kuwait. My mentor is an extremely charismatic leader. He is also a genuine leader. He is passionate. I asked him to define leadership. I remember him pausing on the call to think about the question. At the time of the interview, he was preparing to retire as a Colonel with nearly 30 years in the Army. He had been a leader nearly his whole life. He did not have an answer ready for the question, but when he did answer, it hit home.

Leadership is motivating people to do what they would not do on their own.

The statement is simple, but it holds a lot of power. We can manage people who are doing things they want to. Leading people requires more. I can manage the process. If I manage a process well, I may be able to observe the process with minimal to no intervention. Leaders work to establish the process. Leaders build the team that executes the process and gives them the support that they need to be successful.

WHO?

When we look at leadership, there are so many "who" questions we can ask to help us define leadership. Who is a leader? Who is being led? Who needs the support of a leader? Who wants to be a leader? Who benefits from leadership? There are a lot of ways we can frame the questions to dig deeper into the people who lead and the people who are led.

I like to start with the question – Who is a leader? The question sounds simple when we first ask the question. The person in charge is the leader. But is the person in charge the leader? Is there anyone in the group that people look to for an answer before they respond to the person in charge?

In the Army, we often joked about the E-4 Mafia. When Soldiers reach the rank of Specialist, which is the grade E-4, they are in a position where a lot of new Soldiers begin to look up to them. The Soldiers have typically been in the Army long enough to understand the system and how things work. BUT they have not been promoted to a rank that denotes leadership. The Soldiers know how to get things done. They also know how to get away with things. The E-4 Mafia can be a powerful asset to a leader OR a huge hindrance for the leader. New Soldiers look up to the E-4 Mafia. The E-4 Mafia is imparting the lessons they learned to the new Soldiers. They are creating their next generation. The E-4 Mafia is full of leaders who do not have the title of leader.

We can break leaders into two different categories: Formal and Informal Leaders. Formal Leaders have been designated with a leadership role in the organization. Managers, Directors, Vice Presidents, C-Suite leaders, we can easily recognize formal leaders. Someone else tells us that the person we are looking at is the leader. We often see pictures of the leaders to help us identify the person that we are looking at as a leader. In the Army, we would have the chain of command on a wall within

10

the unit showing each commander and senior non-commissioned officer all the way up to the president. The focus on formal leaders was to identify who is responsible for making decisions within the organization.

Formal leaders have an established level of authority that comes with the position that they hold. Formal leaders may have hiring and firing authority. They may have established authority to spend organizational funds. They may even have the authority to commit the organization in contracts, deals, mergers, and sales.

Formal leaders have responsibilities that they are expected to uphold. Formal leaders must match the authority they hold with responsibility to the organization. If a formal leader has the authority to hire and fire employees, they must be held accountable for hiring the right employees and firing the wrong employees. Organizations entrust leaders with authority to move the organization forward. If the leader does not move the organization forward, they are not meeting the responsibility that is commensurate with the authority.

Informal Leaders are leaders within an organization that do not have authority given to them by the organization. Informal leaders gain their authority from soft power within the organization. People look up to the informal leader. Informal leaders are typically experts, specialists, or they have a charisma that draws people in around them.

Working with informal leaders

Who are experts and specialists is a little different than working around informal leaders who draw people in with charisma.

When we look at the expert informal leader, we look at someone who staff, and formal leadership will turn to because of the knowledge the person possesses. In a lot of the organizations that I have been in, the lawyers are the expert informal leaders. I have heard many formal leaders make a statement like "lawyers don't make decisions, leaders make decisions." The same leaders making the statement will avoid making a decision that the lawyers tell them will put them into hot water. While that expert does not have the authority to make the decision, they guide the formal leader in making the decision.

The specialist informal leader is someone who helps drive the overall system. This can be someone who processes a specific type of transaction in your organization. This can be someone in the IT or HR department who keeps the organization running the way everyone expects it to run. The specialist is good at what they do. People often avoid upsetting or getting on the wrong side of the specialist. It may not be that the specialist is doing things the best way possible, but they have the ability to make things very uncomfortable if their needs aren't being met. Often times, the specialist is the person that people hope never leaves the organization because no one knows how we would replace them.

The expert and the specialist are similar with regards to how they develop informal power. We typically treat them the same way as well. We want to run things by them before we make changes. We want to be on good terms with them socially. We also want to make sure that their needs are met. Long term planning for the organization, we also want to make sure that if they ever need to be replaced it is well planned out with a transition plan.

The charismatic informal leader is unique in how they derive their power. A charismatic informal leader generates power because people like them and want to be on their good side. The charismatic informal leader draws people to them. When you think back to friend groups that form in school, there is often a leader within the different groups. People unanimously accept that someone is in charge of the group without conscious effort.

When we talk about the E-4 Mafia, a lot of the power is derived from the charisma of one of the Soldiers. There is an informal leader for the E-4 Mafia. Soldiers who do not agree with that leader often find themselves on the outside of the group. They are not able to connect with the group in the same way as everyone else.

When we are working with charismatic informal leaders, we need to be conscious of the following that they have. Understand the dynamic that is created around the leader. Is it temporary and more about choosing the right spot for lunch or is it the power to join together and overthrow established management? Does the leader know that they are leading the group or are they unaware of the effects that they are having on the group at large?

The second most important "who" question we need to ask is Who is being led? When we evaluate the who of leadership, we are developing a map of our organization. "Who is the leader?" establishes the chain of command up, down, and sideways from our position. When we ask, "who is being led?", we are looking at the person who is following.

Earlier I highlighted the statement that my mentor shared with me. Leadership is motivating people to do what they would not do on their own. In order to effectively need, you need to know who you are leading.

Different people have different requirements from leaders. Some people will do the work required of them without ever complaining about the leadership. Other people will complain every step of the way regardless of the type of leadership that they receive.

One of the tricks to leadership is eliciting the best out of people and inspiring them to do what they would not do on their own. Some people are inclined to do some tasks, but not others. When we look at who is being led, we need to understand their background, experience, motivational style, likes, dislikes, and what they are most interested in. Developing a connection with the people you lead will help you understand what tools you need when working with those people. The higher you are in the leadership chain, the less you may know each person under your leadership. Creating a connection with the leaders who work for you will help bridge that gap.

WHAT?

When we know who is being led, we can shift our focus to the next W. What. What? What is a leader? What is leadership? What makes a leader? What drives a leader? What is a follower? What makes people follow? There are a lot of ways we can put leader, leadership, follower, or follow into a what statement to better define leadership.

What are we trying to understand with our what question? Who gave us a focus on the person. What shifts our focus to the concept itself.

We are looking to define leadership more holistically when we look at what makes a leader.

What is leadership? I go back to my mentor's statement. Leadership is motivating people to do what they would not do on their own. Leadership is tied to motivation. It is not the process. It is the motivation that initiates the process. Leadership uses tools to motivate people into actions that they would not typically do on their own.

I have four kids. I have to motivate them to do different things around the house that they would not normally do on their own. Each child has different chores that are required of them. When I evaluate the question "what is leadership?" I need to look at the tools I use to motivate my children.

I can always yell at my children to complete a chore they have been assigned. It is not an effective tool in the toolbox though. Yelling gets action completed at that very moment, but the only motivation is to end the yelling.

I can bribe my children. My son, the youngest, loves to play Mario on the Nintendo Switch. It is one of his favorite things. I can bribe him to do a simple chore with the promise of Mario

15

time. In order to bribe my son, I need to be able to pay him though. I cannot bribe him if we do not have the time to play. He also learns that specific rewards may be tied to specific actions.

When I look at a sustainable leadership model with my kids, I need something that motivates the children to do what my wife and I need them to do, when it needs to be done. Yelling and bribery may be tools in the toolbox, but they cannot be the full framework we use to lead our kids.

I used the example of my kids to highlight the need for a leadership framework to simplify leadership into a model we have all experienced. Everyone has at least been a child even if they don't have experience having children. When we look at leadership in an organization, the most basic premises stay the same. We want to motivate people to do what needs to be done.

In the Army, I had the opportunity to go through Air Assault School. It was a fantastic opportunity where some very skilled leaders motivated us to rappel out of a helicopter with ropes that we tied around our waist. There is an immense amount of leadership that is required to motivate someone to rappel out of a helicopter. Everyone was excited about the opportunity, but it is scary. You are up in the air. The ropes you are going to rappel down are moving from the air generated by the blades of the helicopter. It is not like rappelling down a tower where the person on the ground can arrest your fall. Before you rappel out of the helicopter, the leadership teaches you how to create the "slide for life" instead of the previous belay procedure.

It sounds like a lot, but the leaders had to create a framework where we were able to set our fear aside and trust that they had taught us everything we needed to know, would keep us safe, and that we would be better off after finishing the task. It was incredible. The leadership was motivating us to overcome the objections we had in our minds.

When we move our mindset to identifying leadership in our workplace, the framework is more complex than children and hopefully less extreme than rappelling out of helicopters. When we dive deeper into "what is leadership?", we can see that leadership is often tied to management. In the who section, I talked about Managers, Directors, Vice Presidents, and C-Suite leaders as leaders. We expect managers to lead. Not all managers are leaders though. As we looked at in the who section, not all leaders are in management roles.

We can look at two different concepts: management and leadership.

Management is process-focused. Managers are concerned with how the process is conducted and how efficiently the process works. A manager will take a system focus on the tasks that need to be completed. Managers will look at:

- Costs – How much am I spending to generate the product? Is it too much? How can I reduce the costs?
- Time – How much time does it take to generate the product? Can I decrease the time?
- Quality – Is the product of acceptable quality? Should I increase quality?
- Reporting – Are the required reports being generated? Are the right people getting the reports?
- Tasks – Are tasks getting checked off the list? Are there tasks missing from the process? Do we have too many tasks in the process?

Managers are process-focused. Interactions with people are part of managing the process that the manager is focused on. Project managers look at the completion of a specific project. Store managers are focused on the operations of the store. Safety managers are focused on the safety operations.

Leadership is human-focused. Leaders are concerned with the motivation, safety, and quality of the people that they have on their team. A leader will focus on what the team needs to be successful. Leaders will look at:

- Motivation – Is the team motivated to complete the task? If motivation is low, how do I increase motivation? If motivation is high, how do I maintain motivation?
- Safety – Is my team safe in the operation? How can I ensure everyone gets home at the end of the day?
- Training – Does the team have the training they need to be successful? Would they be more successful with more training? Is there training that can be delayed until it is not a distraction?
- Needs – Does the team have everything they need to be successful?
- Growth – Where does each member of the team want to go in their career? How can I help my team grow to their potential?

Leaders focus on the individuals within the team. Interactions are focused on ensuring the team has what is needed to be successful. Managers can be leaders. Leaders can manage. Not everyone is great at both. Both leadership and management require skillsets to be successful. Leaders who also manage have to balance the requirements of the process with the requirements of the team. Balance does not require that equal attention is paid to process and team at the same time. Balance requires that when one aspect needs more attention, the focus is shifted to the appropriate function.

WHERE?

We have looked at who leaders are. We have looked at what leadership is. Now we are diving into the "where" of leadership. Where do we find leaders? Where do leaders come from? Where do leaders start?

Where do we find leaders? Leaders can be found just about everywhere we look.

- Teachers
- Parents
- Coaches
- Management
- Military Leaders
- Political Figures
- Religious Leaders
- Community Volunteers

The list can continue for a long time. We can find leaders in most situations. Not all leaders are created equal. A lot of times we can look around and point out bad leaders. Bad leaders may be easier to identify than good leaders. When we think about leaders, we highlight the ones that are visible. The media does a great job of focusing on areas that need reform, but often glosses over things that are going well.

When I think about leaders that I have interacted with, I often focus on negative experiences I had with the leader. It is easier for me to recall negative experiences with a lot of leaders than positive ones. How many people do you know who have said "when I'm a parent, I won't do what my parents did"? How many times have you thought "when I'm in charge I will not do it the way that my boss does it!" When we're looking for leaders, we get caught up in visible situations and can get wrapped up in the negative things a leader does.

Years ago, I was living in Kentucky, and I went to Louisville for a tour on the bourbon trail. I heard one of the best I'll show you stories that define how people build their leadership styles. Whether the story is true or not, I'm not sure. The owner of Bulleit Whiskey had a job when he was younger putting labels on whiskey bottles. He was constantly getting criticized for putting labels on crooked. He swore that when he owned his own distillery, he would put all of the labels on crooked. Thus, was born the slanted label on Bulleit Whiskey bottles.

We are discussing where leaders come from, and I'm going down a path about bad leaders and putting labels on whiskey bottles crooked. What does that have to do with "where do we find leaders?" I'm glad you asked. We can find leaders everywhere. When we model our leadership style, it is easy to focus on what we will not do that we have learned from poor leaders. By looking for positive leaders around us, we can model the positive tools our good leaders use. It may not be as readily apparent because it does not draw the same frustration from us as poor leadership, but if we are observant, we can find models to emulate.

We know where to look for leaders.

Where do leaders come from? There are a lot of leaders that fill our lives. How do people become the leaders in our lives? Education and experience are the primary selection criteria for leaders.

Education is a great starting point for leaders who are entering into a career. Education is used as a foundation for leadership selection in different industries.

Military – Officers must possess a bachelor's degree to be selected.

Education – Teachers must possess a degree and typically have passed certification exams.

There are other professions that require degrees to be a leader within the profession. When I joined the Army, I entered as an officer. I used the ROTC program at my university to pay for my degree and jump-start my career. An interesting thing I found in the Army was that what your degree was in did not affect the role that you were assigned. The requirement was the degree itself.

Education is used as a requirement in some organizations for leadership roles because it represents an investment in advancement. When you invest in yourself through education, you are telling others that you are willing to spend the time, money, and effort to become more proficient in what you are doing.

Education has the benefit of compressing lessons that have been learned over time by many individuals into a shorter timeframe. Time invested in learning also has the benefit of presenting theories that can be applied. Leadership education comes in different forms. Each form has different benefits that it brings to the leader. The cost behind each form is different as well. Education can look like:

- College
  - Associate's degree
  - Bachelor's degree
  - Master's degree
  - PhD
- Certifications
  - Industry Specific
  - In conjunction with a university
  - In conjunction with a trades program
- Workshops
  - Company Specific

- o Industry Specific
- o Open Programs
- Self-Improvement
  - o Books
  - o Journals
  - o Coaching

There is no one right type of education to help leaders advance in their career. Experience is the other determinant of leader selection. It's easy to select leaders who have previously been successful in leadership roles. We often see leaders who are selected because they are great at the work that they do. The best operator is selected to be the leader.

Experience in the task performed does not always equate to the experience necessary to lead others in the task. The idea behind selecting the best at a task to lead others in the task is simple. If you can do it well, you know what others need to do to do it well. The problem is that leadership comes with additional responsibilities that are not as simple as getting others to repeat the task that you have been good at.

When people are promoted into leadership roles, they are given authority and responsibility. Balancing authority and responsibility when others are executing the work is challenging. You are shifting the dynamic from ownership over the work you are completing to being responsible for the work that others are completing.

I had a manager who worked for me at a company that provided internet service. Construction would move through an area, and then when new customers would sign up, we would send technicians out to install the customer. Part of the process involved running a cable from the main line to the customer's home. When the technicians would run the cable underground, we would often have pipes that the cable could run through from the main line to the customer's property. Sometimes the cable could not get through the pipe to the customer's property. This would stump some of the technicians. The technicians would spend over an hour trying to force the cable through, repushing the cable, and repeating steps. Finally, the technicians would call the manager.

"How many feet did the cable go into the pipe?" He would ask the same question each time. He knew where and how to troubleshoot the problem if he had the answer to that question. The technicians often didn't have that answer. While the manager knew that you needed to answer that question to solve the problem, it took him time as a manager to know that he had to teach the problem-solving skills to the new technicians. There were two sets of skills needed. He needed time as a manager to develop the skill of teaching the work.

Understanding how leaders are selected within your organization can help you understand the steps you need to take to be selected for leadership within your organization. Education can help provide a framework for leadership. Experience can give you tools to fall back on in leadership. Knowing when to use education and when to use experience can be challenging. Often, people lean on the familiar to solve problems and miss other options for solving the problem.

WHEN?

We know who leads. We know what leadership is. We know where to find leaders. "When" sets our next set of questions. "When" is an interesting approach to the leadership toolbox.

- When do leaders take charge?
- When do leaders change the tools they use?
- When do we need a leader?

When do leaders take charge? They do so when they recognize a leadership gap or when they are asked to step into the position. The timing for leaders to take charge depends on the situation.

Leaders take charge when the time is right. Sometimes, leaders are appointed, and other times, leaders have to look around and make the decision to step up and fill a gap.

Leaders appointed to the position will fill the position as soon as they are moved into the role. Sometimes the leader will have the opportunity to work with an outgoing leader to identify a path to taking over the leadership role. The leader will observe what is going on and take transition the responsibility from the outgoing leader to the new leader.

Often, leaders are encouraged to limit changes within the first 30, 60, and 90 days of leadership. The organization needs time to adapt to the new leader. Major changes to the organization can throw the balance off and make it hard for the organization to understand the vision and direction the organization is taking. In the Army, every change of command ceremony I attended ended with the phrase "all policies and procedures remain in effect." The new leader communicated to the field that they did not need to worry about everything changing.

24

There are always exceptions to rules. If the organization is in crisis when the leader is brought in, changes may be needed immediately. Leadership in crisis requires a different level and type of communication to manage the crisis. Leaders brought in to lead through a crisis are selected because they are thought to be well-suited to solving the problem at hand.

When leaders are not appointed but step in to fill a gap, they will typically start making decisions based on the environment. Informal leaders are great at taking charge and filling leadership gaps. Informal leaders recognize that people need to move effectively to make things happen. We see informal leaders step in when the primary leader is out of the loop for a period of time, and the acting leader is overwhelmed filling two positions. The informal leader recognizes the need for support and interjects at the right time.

We also see leaders jump in to fill a gap in short-term team structures. Students in school are often assigned to group work. Without complete democracy in the group, someone is needed to give direction and set the stage for completing the task. Some teams appoint the leader, but others, a leader takes charge.

When do leaders change the tools they use? The short answer is when they need to. Leaders take time developing their toolbox so that they have the best tool for each situation they encounter. Leadership requires constant balance. Leaders need to use tools that balance:

- Individual needs and task completion
- Time to learn and time to achieve
- Flexibility and structure
- Outcomes and hours
- Who gets attention
- Remote, hybrid, and on-site work
- Scheduled hours and flexible hours

Leaders are decision-makers. We expect leaders to prioritize for success. Leaders need to adjust the tool they are using to find the right balance for the organization. Some situations will require higher emotional intelligence. Other situations will require a firmer approach to a situation. Some people require frequent feedback to feel like they are on the right track. Others will feel micromanaged if their leader is constantly around. Finding the right balance for your team is the challenge. The more tools you have, the more options that are available.

When do we need a leader? I may be biased, but I think we always need leaders. We can find a leader in just about any situation. When I'm at home with my wife and kids, we need someone to lead the family. My wife and I find leadership roles that fit one of us better, and we focus on leading our family based on that structure.

In most environments, we can point to a leader and clearly identify who is in charge. Businesses have a management structure that indicates who is in charge at each level. Government has established leaders at each level. We can find leaders within our religious institutions.

If we can find leaders everywhere we look, it stands to reason that we need leaders within our lives. We need to make sure that we align with the right leaders at the right time. What does that mean?

It is important to surround ourselves with the people who help guide us in the right direction. Leaders are decision-makers. If a leader is making decisions that do not align with the decisions you believe are right for you, you need to make sure that you distance yourself from that leader and find a better leader. We do not want our children to surround themselves in a friend group that encourages vandalism, drugs, and petty crime. Someone is leading that group of children. We would pull our children from the group and surround them with more positive influences. If we find ourselves surrounded by leaders who are making risky, dangerous, or unethical decisions, we need to pull ourselves from the situation. There is always someone encouraging the behavior of a group. Our friend group is a reflection of who we are and how we want to be led. Our work environment affects our professional reputation. Knowing when you are being led can help you make conscious decisions for improving your situation.

WHY?

Our last W to consider is why. There are lots of whys. There is a principle called the 5 Whys. Ask "why?" 5 times.

- Why am I reading about leadership? (1)

Because I want to improve my leadership skills.

- Why? (2)

So, I am prepared to lead my team.

- Why? (3)

Because I want my team to succeed.

- Why? (4)

So, we are recognized as the best.

- Why? (5)

So, we can all advance in the organization! Promotions!

When we ask "why?", we are looking for the motivating factors. Digging deeper with why opens the door to a personal conversation with ourselves. Why do we want to lead? Why do we want to learn about leadership? Why? Why? Take it to the fifth why, and we start digging deeper into our motivation.

My why is a passion for helping others succeed. When I joined the Army, the topic of toxic leadership was a big discussion. People were experiencing and talking about the effects of negative leadership. Negative leadership creates an environment where no one can succeed.

I look at leaders who are thrown into leadership roles without the tools necessary to succeed. How can I invest in those leaders and help the next generation of leaders be successful? If I can help a leader be successful, I believe they can pass on the skills to the next generation.

When we examine our own "why?", it inspires us to look at the "how".

ASSEMBLING YOUR TOOLBOX (WHAT DO YOU NEED?)

It is time to consider what tools you will need to put in your toolbox. Leadership looks different for everyone. The way our personalities influence us plays a role in how we respond as leaders. The experiences we have prior to becoming a leader shape the way we respond as leaders. The experience we gain in leadership affects the way we respond as leaders.

We need to identify the tools that we put in our toolbox and how to use them. It's great to have amazing tools. If you do not know how to use the tool, it is about the same as not having it. It would be like buying a top-of-the-line router and not knowing that you need to clamp down what you are working on. You will get an effect from the router, but you won't get the desired effect.

You may be wondering what the toolbox has to do with leadership. Leadership is a craft. When we do a craft, we need to have the right tools to complete the work. Carpenters will have woodworking tools in their toolbox. Mechanics will have automotive tools in their toolbox. Some of the tools will look similar and operate the same way. Other tools will be foreign from one trade to the next.

When we fill our toolbox, we need the tools that apply to us. I don't need tools that I can't use. I look for tools that are adaptable, but I always look to see if there are tools that are a better fit than adapting a tool for another purpose. I have to evaluate the cost to obtain a new tool before I grab it. Does the cost match the need for a new tool, or should I look at adapting a different tool I already have?

The best part about assembling your toolbox is that you are to select tools that you are more naturally inclined to use. If you decide to try a tool that you are less familiar with, it may be uncomfortable, but it has the potential to expand your horizon in tools that you want to use.

Many of the tools we put into our toolbox look at the amount of leadership capital we need to spend in order to achieve the effect we are looking for. When we look at achieving a specific result in a leadership scenario, there are a lot of ways we can approach the situation and achieve the same result. We need to understand the tools in our toolbox to understand what the cost will be for using each of the tools.

When I was in the Army Reserves, my company was tasked with an incredible undertaking that felt like an impossible challenge. The company was already preparing for a month-long training exercise. We received guidance that with an additional train-up and certification from our battalion, we would be tasked with participating in a live fire exercise when we were at the month-long training exercise. Overall, it sounded like a great opportunity, the downside is that we were a reserve unit with 6 weeks prior to the month-long exercise. We had 1 scheduled weekend. There was no way we could complete the exercise in the time we had allotted. We were issued orders that called us all in to complete the training. I had over 100 Soldiers that were pulled away from their normal lives to participate in an unscheduled training. Some Soldiers were thrilled with the prospect of participating in a live-fire exercise. Some Soldiers were missing important classes in their college education. We had Soldiers missing out on work. Most of the Soldiers, myself included, had families at home that planned to miss us for a month in the future, not the time we were missing out on now.

The orders we had were for about a week and a half. We took to the challenge with vengeance. Soldiers were working long hours. We had issues with critical supplies, but Soldiers kept finding ways to succeed. The odds were stacked against success from the beginning. A helpful note in understanding the chaos that we were embroiled in; I had only been in charge of the company for a few weeks when we received the notification that we were being assigned to complete the additional training.

As we were nearing the end of the additional training time, we were not complete on all of the tasks we needed to complete. We had the option to extend our orders and keep training or we could give up and say with all honesty that we had given it our all. We did our best, was it time for us to acknowledge defeat?

As a leader, I had to decide how we would proceed. I needed to throw in the towel or extend everyone's orders to accomplish the mission. It was a decision I was fully responsible for. I would be leading these same Soldiers in the month-long training in less than a month at this point. There were so many questions:

- Can we accept not participating in the live fire after all of our hard work? (Acknowledging the work already completed)
- Can we ask everyone to stay in the field after knowing they would get home? (Acknowledging the sacrifice, they would need to make)
- How do we break the news to everyone?

I spoke with my leaders who worked with and for me. We were all committed to success. We did not want to stay in the field, but we knew that our success would shape the way the battalion trained in the future. We ultimately decided to keep the company in the field, but we would allow Soldiers to leave if they had other commitments and could not stay.

We pulled the team together and I broke the news to them. In breaking the news to the team there were a lot of tools that I needed to use. I had a great team of individuals who had been pulled from their lives with very little input and I needed to convince them to stay.

I had very little leadership capital to spend at this point in my tenure with my team. Leadership capital is how much you can ask people to be uncomfortable and take action that they would not normally take. Routine tasks take little to no leadership capital; the team will complete these actions even if there is no boss who is managing their work.

When there is no leadership capital and the leader has a big request for the team, the check bounces and the task is at risk of failure. A boss who is too authoritarian and never looks for input from the team is at risk of having team members quit because he has no leadership capital left to spend. Micromanaging bosses run out of leadership capital.

When leadership capital is high, a boss can ask the team to complete nearly any task and the team will jump at the

33

opportunity. Leaders with high leadership capital invest in the team and are repaid well. The team wants the leader to succeed.

Leadership capital is not stagnant. Leaders can gain and lose leadership capital based on the actions they take. It is like a bank account. Our interactions with others are transactions that we make. Some transactions use up capital. Other transactions put deposits in the bank. Leaders don't need to try to own the bank. Leaders need to make sure they keep putting a little away for a rainy day. Invest in your team to ensure that you can produce results tomorrow.

Earlier in the book we talked about formal and informal leaders. Formal leaders typically start off with a fixed level of leadership capital. The amount is based on the level of authority that the leader holds. The starting amount can be affected by the previous leader in the role. If the previous leader created a toxic climate, the team may require a lot of convincing to achieve any task. Or the team may respond with the opposite reaction and appreciate any gesture. If the previous leader was a phenomenal leader, the team may jump to help out at every opportunity. The team may also have high expectations and it may take more work to develop the leadership capital. The rate that we build the capital is dependent on where we are. But we can use similar tools to build capital.

With very little leadership capital I had to use different tools to convince my team to stay when they wanted to go home. I could have told everyone that we were out of options and had to stay for the extra time required to complete the mission. I could have said it was out of my hands, the exercise was being extended. Both options would not have built leadership capital with the company. The first option would demonstrate that I did not have any emotional intelligence or empathy for the company. I would have demonstrated a high focus on task and virtually no focus on the Soldiers. The second option is equally bad. I would have removed myself as a leader and demonstrated that I am a figurehead who is not responsible for decisions. While I would look like a weak leader, it would still look like I place tasks over Soldiers.

I owned the decision to stay. I let everyone know that if they had commitments that did not allow their orders to be extended, I would not hold anything against them and neither would their fellow Soldiers. I gave an impassioned speech. I spoke about the struggles we had faced and the reachability of our goal. I highlighted the confidence that leadership had in our ability to complete the goal with a few extra days. I spoke of my feelings about spending additional time in the field. I put myself in their shoes. I appealed to different motivations – pride of being the first engineer company to have the achievement, success in participating in the live fire, the dedication from their team, and my pride in what we have already accomplished. I let the company know that I was putting them and the task at the same level, 100% of my focus. I spoke to every Soldier together. Every part of my company was there. When I was done, I couldn't remember the words I had spoken, but they came from the heart. Nothing was prepared in advance. I spoke from the heart with genuine conviction. I believe 1 Soldier had to leave, but the remaining company was not only ready to stay, but they were also motivated to stay.

I had built leadership capital with my company while sharing bad news.

In leveraging tools from my toolbox, I had built leadership capital with my team. In building the toolbox, we look for tools that resonate with us and engage the teams that we are working with. Some organizations are used to leaders who give direction and never seek input from their teams. The turnover in those teams is often high because people run out of reasons to stay.

There are 4 groups of tools we will take a look at for our toolboxes:

- Emotional Intelligence
- Empathy
- Motivation
- Engagement Frameworks

These tools are the foundation for everything else we will explore. Emotional intelligence, empathy, motivation, and engagement serve as the basic tools we will use in different applications as we progress. Each tool helps to shape the way that our toolbox is formed.

I spent time wearing a toolbelt doing rough framing, remodeling, and a few side projects. There were a few tools that I could not go to work without. I always had a hammer, tape measure, square, and pencil. I usually had a chalk line, a few nail sets, and other tools in my belt, but I could not show up to work without the basic tools in my toolbelt.

When we show up to work as a leader, we need to have our basic tools in our toolbox that enable us to be successful. Regardless of whether I was on a rough framing project or a remodel site, I needed a hammer to get the job done. It may not be as quick as the nail gun, but it could do more for me than the nail gun. Emotional intelligence, empathy, motivation, and engagement are those same core tools. They are not always the tools we will use, but they are tools we cannot go to work without.

EMOTIONAL INTELLIGENCE

What is emotional intelligence? For many of us, emotions get in the way of intelligence. We think with our brain, and we feel with our heart. How can emotions be intelligent?

Emotional intelligence is understanding how your words and actions will affect yourself, others, and ultimately help you shape the way people react to you. Developing a fundamental understanding of emotional intelligence focuses on 4 areas:

1. Self-Awareness
2. Self-Control
3. Relationship Awareness
4. Relationship Management

Self-Awareness is understanding how you feel when you feel it.

Have you ever had a talk with someone and during the conversation, you really didn't have much of a reaction, but as you walk away from the situation, you start to get really upset? You may be angry about the way the person spoke to you. You may be upset about the person not being supportive of you. You may be hurt that you were not heard.

We don't always pay attention to what we feel in the moment that we feel it. It is easy to neglect how we are feeling in the moment and find ourselves reacting before we ever recognize that we have even had time to make a decision.

I know I have had arguments where I didn't realize I was angry until I heard my own voice yelling. In situations like this, it is easy to dismiss your own feelings and recognize them as a product of the situation and not a product of our own emotions. When a situation escalates before we recognize our own emotions, it can be really disconcerting.

Building self-awareness is a process. We want to get our awareness to real-time processing. I never act on my emotions without recognizing that I am feeling an emotion. To get to real-time processing of emotions, you need to reflect on how different situations make you feel. It takes time, and you may not always have the answer for how you feel.

Take time throughout your day and ask yourself, "how did that make me feel?" You can start building a baseline of how you feel when you encounter different situations. With the baseline, you can feed into the next step, self-control. Look at your day and see how different situations make you feel.

Morning:

- Running out of coffee and realizing you or your spouse didn't buy any
- Getting cut off in traffic
- Being told that you look nice today
- Finding a quarter in the parking lot

Throughout the day:

- Pulled into an unplanned meeting
- Getting praised for work that you submitted
- Receiving group punishment for someone else's failure
- Getting 15 minutes back from a meeting before lunch
- Your friendly coworker disagrees with you

In the evening:

- You have to work late
- Your kids' bus arrives early, before you get there
- Your spouse has a nice dinner waiting for you
- Your favorite movie was just released

There are tons of opportunities to pay attention to how we feel throughout the day. You can then look at whether the situation affects you the same way every day or if there are differences.

Do you find that if one negative thing happens to you, you perceive everything negatively?

Do you find that one positive thing happens, you perceive everything positively?

Does it make a difference with the order things happen to you?

Are you more affected by the scale of what happens than the order of things?

The way we react is unique to us. Understanding how I react before an event allows me to prepare for a situation. As leaders, we will often get thrown a curveball. We are often thrown into situations that we have never dealt with before. We can't always predict how we will react in those situations. We can take the time to understand how we feel about what has happened.

I had a complex situation happen when I was a platoon leader in the Army. I had 32 Soldiers in my platoon that I was responsible for. On Friday, I commented about the unbelievable potential of one of my Soldiers. He was dedicated, talented, and always willing to volunteer for any task. Sunday morning, he called me from jail to let me know that he was not going to be released without cash bail or until after it had been heard by a judge. He had 5 charges tied to not keeping his alcohol use under control. My initial reaction was disappointment and sadness. I was disappointed that he would put himself in that position. I was sad that there would be additional consequences for a lapse in judgment. I began to feel a little betrayed. I considered him a top Soldier, and after praising him, he got himself in trouble. I then began to feel resolved to help and support my Soldier. My platoon sergeant and I discussed the situation and came up with an action plan.

Monday morning, my platoon sergeant and I were ready to head to the police station to support our Soldier and see if we could convert his bail to a bond. We were set to head out after the first formation, BUT we had a second Soldier who missed formation. We had to find this Soldier before we could help the first Soldier. The second Soldier had caused issues in the past, but he was part of our team. At this point, the frustration was high. We searched and searched and searched before running out of places to check. We decided to head to the jail and see what we could figure out.

We succeeded in changing the bail to a bond, had a bondsman there to get the Soldier out, and my platoon sergeant's phone rang. All I heard was laughter on the other side. The second Soldier had been found. In the cell next door to the first Soldier.

That had a lot of emotions. There was some comic relief, some overall disappointment, and a little fear over the repercussions that the whole unit would face for 2 alcohol-related arrests in the same weekend. I am aware of a lot of feelings that I felt between Friday and Monday morning.

So why does it matter how we feel?

Self-Control is the second part of emotional intelligence. When I understand how I feel, I can ask myself what the best response is before I respond.

When we have the baseline of how we feel, we can better prepare for situations we know are coming and better evaluate our reactions when an unplanned situation arises.

Does my reaction seem out of the ordinary? When we encounter an event that we have experienced before, does our reaction match what we normally see?

If I normally get mildly frustrated at being cut off in traffic and today, I'm raging mad, I can self-evaluate to say that my reaction is not normal. When I recognize that my reaction is not within normal ranges, I can focus on the actions I take because of my reactions.

As a parent, I have days where I may be frustrated from work or from having to run around for most of the afternoon, when the kids start arguing I may be more sensitive to the fighting and want to raise my voice or punish them. I will be more inclined to choose temporary solutions that may be more aggressive (raising my voice or punishing) rather than helping to resolve the situation. Self-control is recognizing that my reaction may not support the message that I want to send to my children. When I recognize that my frustration is already high, I can make the conscious decision to work with my children in resolving their conflict rather than adding to the conflict in the situation by raising my voice or punishing them.

The inverse situation may also be true. I may be having a great day and find that I am allowing the situation around me to go unattended because I am in a good mood. The situation may lead to my children getting away with more. I urge caution when you are paying attention to your reactions and notice that you do not enforce the rules as well when you are in a positive mood. This has the ability to reduce leadership capital if the team is relying on your mood for when they will comply with the guidance you have given. If you notice that you have positive reactions when you are in a good mood and stay engaged, you have a great baseline for moving forward.

After examining your reactions and establishing a baseline, do you notice trends that you want to change? Do you notice trends you want to reinforce?

When we exhibit self-control, we become the masters (or at least leaders) of our emotions and do not allow them to rule us. Take note of the reactions that you like and dislike and make a positive effort to keep doing what leads to greater positivity and reduce what leads to greater negativity.

One of the hardest concepts in self-control is identifying short-term gratification and long-term gratification. When we allow our emotions to be our masters, we neglect the long-term plan. Gratification comes when we receive a positive reinforcement. Short-term gratification comes from pleasure you can receive in a moment. Long-term gratification comes from achieving a goal that you have planned out. Think about eating junk food when you are on a diet. The junk food tastes great and gives you pleasure in the moment. The big BUT is that junk food delays your goal of reaching a fitness level. On the other side, when temptation is high and we avoid junk food, we are delaying gratification for long-term gratification. Long-term gratification is achieved by being consistent and being focused on the goal. Reaching the desired level of fitness is the long-term gratification we have been seeking. Long-term gratification comes from discipline and hard work. There aren't short cuts to long-term gratification. You have to work at it for a while, but it comes from the achievement of goals we have worked for.

I am really conscious of road rage when I am driving. There are times I would love to lay on the horn, make a gesture, or roll down my window to tell someone what I think of their driving. I don't, though. When I was learning to drive, my dad always cautioned me that you never know who is in the cars around you. It could be the employer you are driving to interview with. It could be your spouse's parents. It could be a crazy person even less worried about my long-term plan than I am.

Simple choices can have long-term consequences. While I used a road rage example, we can easily translate the decision to the workplace. Blowing up on a coworker can create an environment where our coworkers don't want to work with us, our boss thinks we're a liability, and HR knows our name. Asking out a coworker who seems friendly can create a situation where we can no longer work together and worst-case scenario, HR knows our name. Decisions that are tied to emotions often have less thought than the decisions we evaluate from a calm and centered mind.

How many people have heard a narrative about someone who gets drunk at a company function and messes up their career because they had too much fun?

At the root of self-control, we are willing to give up immediate gratification for a longer-term plan. We focus on the actions we take now to evaluate how they will affect us in the future. We then try to make decisions with our longer-term goals.

At this point, I hope you are asking yourself "how does my self-control make me a better leader? I'm focusing on myself."

A leader with self-control is a leader that we can trust to make decisions that are fair and consistent. The consistent part of the statement typically holds more weight than fair. Consistency leads to a concept called procedural fairness. People like to know what the rewards and penalties are. When a leader is inconsistent, you don't know what will happen. Will you get praised or will you get chewed out? With consistency, your team will understand your position and will be better suited to meeting your expectations.

The stability that is offered through self-control will also help you as a leader in your decision-making. Knowing what is driving your decisions will help you reflect on where the decision is coming from and allows you to evaluate whether or not the decision supports your long-term plan.

Relationship Awareness is the third area of emotional intelligence. In our first step, we examined how we feel in a given situation. In our second step, we looked at how we control our reactions to support a long-term plan. Our third step is to examine the reactions of others.

This is the part of leadership that a lot of historical leadership styles neglected. Historically leaders lead and followers follow. Whether leaders were natural born leaders, divinely selected, or ruled due to their strength, the reactions of others were considered secondary to the command of the leader. Where is the place in leadership for this touchy-feely approach to others where we have to worry about people's emotions and feelings? Does paying attention to feelings mean I need to cater to the emotions of others?

It is a lot easier to lead people who want you to succeed than it is to force a group to submit to your commands long term. You may be able to succeed for a while, but eventually you will run out of leadership capital and will have a stream of new team members to lead or a small team because you cannot keep anyone on the team.

Leadership is built on relationships. Earlier we discussed formal and informal leadership. Informal leaders derive soft power from relationships. Understanding the reactions of others is a huge part of leadership. Organizations devote resources to the relational side of the organization to protect themselves from liability and maintain a healthy working environment.

Every organization I have ever been a part of has had programs in place to prevent harassment and discrimination. Harassment and discrimination are often the result of a message conveyed not translating to the message received. One individual may make a comment that is intended to be a harmless comment that another individual deems to be offensive. Organizations provide harassment and discrimination training to open people up to other perspectives. Their original perspective is not the only perspective. New perspectives reduce the chance that they act in a way that upsets those around them.

There is a scene from the Drew Carey Show from years that highlights how a "harmless" joke can create a lot of drama in the workplace. Drew Carey had a comic that he posted in his cubical. The comic displayed a caterpillar climbing on top of a French fry and trying to mate. The French fry tells the caterpillar to knock it off; it's a French fry. The comic was intended to be funny. Drew and his friends found it funny. Others in the office did not. There was a dispute about the comic because it created a hostile workplace.

There are two conflicting perspectives in the story. Drew made a decision he felt was harmless. Someone else was offended. As a result, the whole situation became difficult to manage.

As leaders, we need to understand how those around us are reacting and understand how they may react. Similar to evaluating our reactions, we want to understand how our team members will react to different situations. Note the distinction between team members and the team in this situation. The team may collectively react in a unified manner, but individual team members may have reactions that do not align with the group reaction.

How do team members react to notice that they are needed for overtime work?

- Anger?
- Joy?
- Neutral?

- Frustration?

What motivates the team members to feel that way about overtime? Do they have a family waiting for them at home? Do they need the money? Are they just happy to have job security? Are they frustrated with the overtime or the timing of the notice? There are a lot of drivers in a reaction. Understanding not only how a person feels but why they feel that way will help us when we move to the next step.

Not everything will apply to your team, but use the list below as a starting point for evaluating your team members' reactions:

- Working overtime
- Performance reviews
- Response to deadlines
- Assigning new tasks
- Positive feedback
- Negative feedback

When you are evaluating your team members' reactions look at their emotional reactions, behavioral reactions, and verbal reactions. Do all of the reactions line up? Do the reactions point to the same conclusion of how the individual is interpreting the event?

It makes sense if they don't all align. As people gain self-control, they do not always display behavioral and verbal reactions that align with their emotional reaction. A team member can be disappointed with working overtime, display no behavioral reaction, and verbally agree to the overtime. An employee can be excited about positive feedback, act timid, and provide no verbal feedback. Multiple truths can apply at the same time. It is working to decipher what the three categories in conjunction with each other mean that gives us insight into the reaction of our team members. We are looking for emotional responses like joy, anger, frustration, happiness, and neutrality. We are looking to see if they react with increased or decreased motivation.

Relationship management is our fourth step in emotional intelligence. When we understand how our team members will react to various situations, we can lead our team through various situations.

If you have a team member who does not react well to performance reviews, you cannot abandon performance reviews for that team member. You need to find a different way to handle the performance reviews in a way that puts the team member at ease.

For short encounters where you need to address a team member's performance you can put the team member at ease by using the sandwich method. Start with a compliment. "You are doing great in engaging your customers. I like that you are reaching out to your customers monthly." Move to an area that needs improvement. "I would like to mention that your projects are consistently running over budget. I believe the overruns are due to underestimating. We need to refine your estimates." After providing the area for improvement, finish with a compliment. "You're a great asset to this team. I'm glad to have you with us." You are framing the situation, so the person enters and leaves the engagement with a positive experience. This should help put the person at ease and help you build rapport with your team members.

In the third step, we discussed understanding the motivations behind the reaction. If you have an employee who does not mind working overtime but consistently gets frustrated when you ask at the end of the day, look at the time that you are asking. The frustration may revolve around the lack of reaction time. Adjusting when we have engagements is an approach to managing reactions.

In our second step, we talked about managing our own reactions when we recognize that our reactions are off. When you see another person getting frustrated about something, that is probably the wrong time to discuss additional tasks, performance, or anything that will require deliberate processing. It may be a great time to casually drop a compliment without further discussion. Provide reinforcement when they are overwhelmed, but do not ask for anything additional.

When we look at relationship management, we want to help others achieve the result that we are looking for. There are a lot of ways we can help others achieve the results that we are looking for. We open the door to understanding what to do when we understand the motivation behind the reaction.

I had a team member whom I could praise for days. He was a great employee—detail-oriented, focused, and also fun to be around. There was only one thing I could fault the guy on. I required my project managers to provide a Gantt chart for their projects. The Gantt chart is a timeline that shows when different work activities will be taking place on a project. This guy was always late submitting updates on his Gantt charts. He would often go weeks at a time without providing updates.

He was my only project manager who worked in the same building as me. I knew he didn't intend to blow me off. He had a heavy workload, but he had the capacity to get the work done. In talking with him, he wasn't comfortable with the way he needed to make the updates. He needed additional training and support to get better information for the updates. I could have just explained the standard and walked away, but his reaction would have been to continue shutting down. By digging into his motivation, I was able to help him reach the results I was looking for.

Relationship management is all about utilizing the information we learn from other reactions to help us shape the way we interact with them. We have to work through all the steps of emotional intelligence to get to where we can successfully implement relationship management. If you don't understand how you react, it will be harder for you to identify how others react. If you cannot control your reactions, how can you guide others in their reactions?

EMPATHY

Empathy is putting yourself in someone else's shoes and looking at things from their perspective. When we look at things from someone else's perspective, we are opening ourselves up and sharing vulnerability with that individual. There are four elements of empathy that can make you more successful:

1. Active listening
2. Validation
3. Do not project
4. No judgment

Active listening is the act of opening yourself up to listen to the person you are speaking with. In active listening, you are making the speaker the subject of your attention. You place the speaker as the focal point.

When we actively listen, we are allowing our focus to shift away from ourselves and transition to someone else. This does a few things for us as leaders:

1. It helps us understand the perspective of the other person because we are limiting the distractions that may cause us to pull our attention away.
2. It builds rapport with the person who is speaking because that person can see that we are engaged.
3. It is a visible indicator that you care about the person who is speaking.

To actively listen, practice the SLANT method. This can be used with large group settings, classroom trainings, or one-on-one engagements.

S- Sit up
L- Lean forward
A- Ask questions

N- Nod your head
1. Track the speaker

The way that we position ourselves has an impact on the way that the person we are speaking to feels about the conversation. I have had countless conversations where I feel like I need to hurry up my side of the conversation because the other person's body language was telling me that they were not fully engaged in the conversation. I took their lack of engagement to be a statement on how I was boring them or pulling them from something they would rather be doing. There are indicators that people can see when we are talking with them.

With the SLANT method, sitting up encourages our bodies to be more alert and signals to the speaker that we are engaged. When we lean forward, we are moving closer to the speaker and taking a position that indicates interest. Leaning back in the chair is a relaxed position that requires minimal effort. Leaning forward is an act that engages the body. Asking questions can be a clear demonstration that you are engaged with what the speaker is saying. If you ask questions that were answered while the speaker was speaking, you may undermine the effectiveness of the step. Ask clarifying questions and detail-oriented questions. The right questions will tell the speaker that you are engaged and want them to keep sharing with you. Nodding your head is an active listening step that acknowledges you are listening to what is being shared. We nod in agreement. Nodding while listening shows that you are absorbing the information being shared. Tracking the speaker is the act of following the speaker with your head and your eyes. Depending on the size of the engagement, eye contact may be the most appropriate way to track the speaker. In larger group settings, following with your head will demonstrate your active listening.

The SLANT method is intended for seated communication, but active listening can occur in any setting. When you are having a conversation with someone and you are standing, have you ever noticed the direction their feet are pointed? When you are fully engaged in a conversation with someone, you are more likely to point your feet towards the person. When you are not engaged, your feet will point away, and you are likely to turn at the waist to converse. It is a subtle note that you will be walking away as soon as the opportunity arises. When actively listening, make sure that your body language indicates that you are fully engaged in the conversation.

Validation in empathy is when you affirm that the other person's perspective is a valid point of view. It does not mean that you have to agree with the person, but you are validating that they have a valid perspective.

In validating someone else's perspective, you are acknowledging their right to their opinion and opening yourself to listening to their perspective.

I had a Soldier that worked for me in the reserves. He was a good Soldier. He put in solid effort when he was at drill, and he always made sure that he completed the tasks he was assigned. He was a college student while serving in the reserves. Our operations' tempo was beginning to increase, and we were finding the unit on orders or long drill weekends more frequently than the unit had previously encountered. The Soldier begin to miss drill weekends without getting the proper approvals prior to the weekend. He was upset that he was missing out on time to study. He was upset that he was falling behind in some of his classes and that he would have training during the middle of the semester and would have to make a choice between withdrawing for a semester due to military hardship, working harder to get ahead, or foregoing his commitment to the unit.

When I spoke with the Soldier about his poor attendance, I was able to validate that he had a hard decision he had to make. I was able to validate that it was not a great position that he was in. I did not have to validate that he was making the right decision. I was willing to work with him to explore his options, but I had to first validate that the position he was in was not one I would want to find myself in.

The Soldier needed to be heard before he could make a decision.

When we provide validation for others, we create a safe space where they can process the issues that they are working through. Adding validation as a tool to our toolbox can be as simple as offering space for people to be heard. Try statements like:

- "I understand why you would feel that way."
- "It's ok to feel that way."
- "I'm here if you want to talk about it."
- "Thank you for sharing your perspective with me."

Validation creates the opening for more dialogue and lets the other person know that you care.

Do not project. This is a sentence by itself. Do not project your thoughts and feelings onto the other person. All of us interact with the world through our own lens. The way we see the world and the way that we perceive the world is unique to each of us. There are overlaps in our perceptions and experiences, but we cannot assume that the person we are speaking to looks at things in the same manner.

In our discussion on validation, I spoke about the Soldier who was struggling with his priorities of college and reserve duty. It would be easy for me as his commander to say that he needs to put the Army first. He made a commitment, and he needs to honor that commitment above all others. As a Soldier, I have missed out on birthdays, holidays, and time that I would rather have spent in other ways.

That projection would not have built trust or narrowed the gap in the opinions that we held. After I validated that his frustration is valid, it would crush the trust we were building for me to tell him how to make the decision he needed to make. He needs to understand the consequences for his decisions, but I cannot force him to look at it from my perspective to come to the decision I believe he needs to make.

In empathy, we need to put ourselves into the shoes of the people we are working with to better understand where they are coming from. I cannot understand my Soldier if I project my life experiences onto the decision that the Soldier needs to make. Instead, I need to put myself into the perspective of the Soldier and look at the situation from that perspective.

Not projecting is probably one of the hardest parts of empathy. When we are empathetic, we are putting ourselves into someone else's perspective and looking at the situation from the other person's point of view. It is extremely easy to put ourselves into someone else's situation but then look at it from our own perspective. To truly be empathetic, we need to put ourselves in someone else's situation and then look at the situation from their perspective. Understanding not only the situation but the way the other person is experiencing the situation is where empathy starts to take place.

When we can avoid projecting, we can begin to understand the choices that other people make.

No judgment is the last of our elements of empathy. When we are talking with someone, we hold all of the judgment to ourselves. It would be unrealistic to say, don't cast any judgment and have no opinion on the situation. You will have a judgment. You will have an opinion. Keep that opinion to yourself unless you are asked for it.

There is a time and place for judgment and opinions. When we are discussing empathy, empathy is judgment-free. We need to keep our judgments to ourselves.

Everyone has an opinion. It is important to understand the environment in which we express our opinion and limit it to the right time and the right place. When we practice empathy, it is neither the time nor the place.

Not sharing our judgment is easier when we can avoid projecting. Judgment is formed from our perspective. When we are being empathetic, we are removing our perceptions from the equation to look at the situation from the other person's perspective.

Looking at the same Soldier who was not showing up to drill, I wanted to tell him he was risking his future career by not meeting his commitments and obligations. I could not do that from a place of empathy, though. I can explain the consequences in a factual way, but my judgment that it is a mistake could not be shared while I was being empathetic. I could share my opinion in a later meeting with the Soldier, but not when he was coming to me as an empathetic listener.

I do not want you to leave this section believing that you cannot have opinions or share them. You absolutely can, but not when you are being empathetic. When we are embracing empathy, we need to cast off the judgment for a time when it is more appropriate.

UNDERSTANDING MOTIVATION

What is motivation? Why does motivation matter? Motivation is the drive to accomplish the task or mission at hand. People with low motivation are not likely to invest the time and effort required to complete the work that we need them to. Understanding what motivates people can help us use the right tools to get people engaged. How many times have you heard about a workplace that works everyone to the bone and then offers a pizza party as if that will erase the memories that people have of being worn out and broken down by the long hours? The pizza party offers people a meal, camaraderie, and a brief break from work; but it does not offer a lasting and tangible benefit to ensure future motivation. While kids in a classroom may get excited about a pizza party as a reward, it doesn't provide a significant reward to an adult in the workplace.

How do we figure out what motivates people? There are three leadership models that focus on motivation: Theory X, Theory Y, and Maslow's Hierarchy. Theory X and Theory Y are two of my favorite theories for how people interact with their workplace. The theories are the opposite of each other. Theory X states that employees are inherently lazy and need to be forced to do anything at work. Theory Y states that employees are intrinsically motivated to work and will seek out work that they find satisfying. In Theory X, managers need to be very controlling. Employees are given very little freedom and often see strict punishments. The use of rewards is high when managers fall into Theory X thinking. Managers must incentivize the work and punish any infraction. In Theory Y, managers are collaborative with their teams. Employees have a high level of freedom where creativity is viewed as a positive trait within the workplace. Managers will often delegate authority to employees in Theory Y thinking because they trust that their employees will do the right thing. Theory X and Theory Y make great anchor points on a spectrum of intrinsic motivation employees feel towards their workplace. When we look at where a person's motivation comes from, we can begin to understand why they put more effort into some tasks than others. Using Theory X as the left side of the scale and Theory Y as the right side of the same scale, we look at the use of tangible rewards versus intangible rewards.

Our employee further to the left is working for the paycheck and does not see value in the work outside of earning a living and providing necessities. The employee is most likely focused on getting through the workday and is not looking at career progression within the organization.

When work is only a means to an end, the motivation required will be externally focused. Employees will be motivated by bonuses, opportunities for overtime pay, free items, and other things that lessen their overall expenses.

Our employee further to the right is working for a purpose. The employee sees their time as an investment that they are making in their own future. By spending time on a task, they are likely to recognize the value that they are bringing to the task and organization.

When work serves an inner purpose, motivation will be internally focused. Employees in this category will be motivated by promotions, public recognition, and opportunities to expand their responsibilities.

Because few of your team members will fit perfectly into either category, it helps to figure out where each of your team members falls in the different categories. The way that you motivate and manage team members will vary from team member to team member.

Motivating team members becomes a matter of meeting that team member's needs where they matter most to that team member. You can also begin to create awareness for how closely you monitor the team member's work. Externally motivated team members will potentially need more supervision than team members who are intrinsically motivated. There is always the opportunity that employees may be motivated externally but require low supervision or be intrinsically motivated but need high motivation. Understanding the motivation provides a starting point for providing the team members with the support they need.

There is another framework that helps us identify the needs of employees: Maslow's Hierarchy of Needs. Maslow's Hierarchy of Needs is a pyramid with 5 levels; physiological at the base, safety at the second level, belonging and love in the middle, esteem just below the top, and self-actualization capping the pyramid.

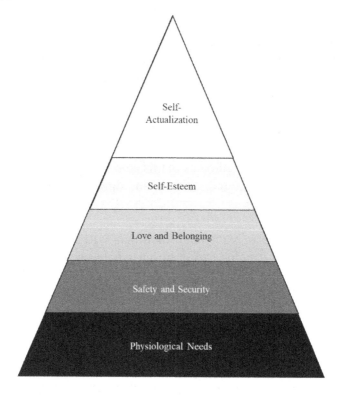

Physiological refers to the physical necessities people have to survive. At a base level, people need food, water, and shelter. Without the most basic necessities, people are not able to survive, much less perform. People will seek out the basic necessities first. When a person has the physiological needs secured, they can begin to worry about securing higher levels of needs within the pyramid.

Team members who are struggling to find the most basic resources will not be in a position to perform. Their primary concern is where their next meal will be coming from, where they will stay, and if they will have power on when they return home. Supporting team members whose motivation is at the physiological level will require helping them find support systems that allow them to meet the most basic needs. If you come across a team member who does not appear to be trying to fulfill the basic needs, you may need to help connect them with support agencies designed to provide help. You can provide support by being a resource for finding the right resources. Investing in team members who are struggling with physiological needs is an investment in their future.

When team members have their physiological needs met, the next level is safety.

Safety involves physical safety, job security, moral safety, family safety, health, and property safety. In general, people do not want to be hurt, lose their jobs, give up their values, or lose what matters most to them.

How do you motivate team members who are focused on safety? These are the team members who are just comfortable that their physiological needs are being met.

Ensure that you are providing a safe environment for them to work in. People may initially resist some safety measures, but seeing people get hurt creates an environment where people become less concerned. Enforcing safety standards ensures that people begin to feel comfortable and safe performing.

Transparency can create safety. Whether you are leading people in the workplace, at home, or in an extracurricular environment, let people know where they stand within the organization. It is terrifying to know that there may be secret layoffs in the future. As a leader, presenting all of the facts will allow your team members to make informed decisions and feel safe in making the decisions. If people cannot find safety where they are, they will look for safety elsewhere.

Following safety is belonging and love. There is a reason that many organizations present themselves as a family. People belong to families. People find love in families.

When people no longer have to worry about finding shelter, food, water, and safety, they can begin to look for a place they belong to.

When motivating team members who are looking for belonging and love, you should find ways to include and bring them into the team. The way someone is welcomed into an organization has a lasting effect on their perception of the organization.

Many of the people who are in the belonging and love level will be recent hires or additions to the organization. The individual is joining the organization because they believe that the organization will provide them with the safety that they are seeking. Once safety is secured, they want to feel like they belong.

There are a lot of ways to give people their own place within the organization. You may look at a special project that they can be a champion for. You may look at inviting the team member to lunch. The organizational culture will help shape the way to bring new people into the organization.

After belonging and love, you can begin to focus on esteem. Does the role provide you with confidence? Respect? A sense of accomplishment?

Esteem is the next level. Once we are accepted into the group, we want to be recognized for the work that we do well. When our team members are no longer new to the organization, they will often fall into this level of the pyramid. This is an area where understanding how the person receives esteem is essential. Some team members will prefer public praise letting them know that they have done well. Others will prefer a private compliment that acknowledges their hard work.

A phrase that I often use is "I appreciate you." I will also say "I appreciate you doing...", but to me "I appreciate you" says more to someone than a longer statement.

"I appreciate you."

It tells the person that I am talking to that it is not just transactional appreciation. It is a way to say that in our engagements, they provide me with value. It implies that a poor-quality task will not reduce the appreciation nor a high-quality task improving it. I appreciate the person for everything they bring.

It can throw some people off, but the concept is simple. It is open gratitude for being someone who makes things better for me. As a leader, gratitude is one of the easiest tools to use. Gratitude builds leadership capital within the team. When people feel appreciated, they are likely to continue supporting.

When team members have esteem within the organization, they can begin self-actualization. This is where people begin to accept the organization for the way that it is and find new ways to contribute. At the top of the pyramid, the team members' needs are met, and they can begin to try things in a new way. Team members may try tackling new problems that they had not been confident to tackle before. They may try a new creative approach when in the past they would not have tried.

In the self-actualization level of needs met, freedom is the best motivator. Team members can try new things, offer new perspectives, and develop a new perspective.

Have you seen the team member that one day steps out of their shell to offer a brand-new perspective? The team member who is typically reserved but, after being recognized as a strong contributor, begins to offer even more to the team. When we foster employee development through the organization, we can see them open up into new and amazing opportunities.

As we look at Maslow's Hierarchy of Needs and compare it back to Theory X and Theory Y, there are parallels. Theory X is easily attributable to someone who is seeking physiological or safety needs. They are not going to go out of their way to find new ways to perform. They are focused on survival. Theory Y is someone who has esteem and is looking for new problems to solve.

There are a lot of ways we can approach motivation, but at the root of the matter, we are looking for where a person is and how we can support them in performing.

ENGAGEMENT FRAMEWORKS

The last focus we will discuss in this chapter is framing out the idea of engagement. Who or what are we looking to engage? When I think of engagement, I always jump to the managerial grid framework. The managerial grid theory was developed by Robert Blake and Jane Mouton in 1964. The theory looks at two dimensions on a graph to figure out what kind of manager you are.

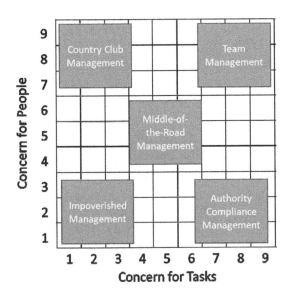

The X-axis or the horizontal dimension on the graph is concern for tasks. Concern for tasks asks the question on a scale from 1-9: How concerned with the tasks are you? When you ask yourself the question, break it down into a few different areas:

- Quantity of tasks produced
- Quality of tasks produced
- Time to produce the tasks
- Cost to produce the tasks

When we focus on our concern for tasks, there are different dimensions that we look at. In a service industry, the number of tasks may be the number of customers served well in a restaurant. In a production facility, the number of tasks may be the number of widgets produced per hour.

A focus on tasks is important to the organization. Even when we look at the family as the organization, there are defined tasks that need to be accounted for to ensure that the needs of the organization's customers are met. Parents cannot run a family without ensuring meals are prepared and kids are ready for school. Organizations exist for a reason. A focus on the task is a focus on the objectives of the organization.

The task focus begins to identify the level of management that the leader is focused on. Higher levels of concern for task indicate higher levels of overall management. Management is different from leadership. Managers can be leaders and leaders can be managers, but the two are distinct concepts.

Managers focus on administrative responsibilities, processes, projects, programs, and systems. Many jobs have a project manager or a construction manager. They have a distinct scope of tasks that they are responsible for managing. Those tasks have outputs that generate revenue for the company or provide societal value in the case of non-profit organizations.

Leaders focus on vision, direction, motivation, and connection. When I go back to the advice of my mentor, leadership is motivating people to do what they would not do on their own. Leadership is the people side of the work that we do where management is the process side. Leaders motivate people to complete the work. Managers keep the work moving. Where the two areas overlap is where managers need leadership skills and leaders need management skills.

When we shift over to the Y-Axis, the vertical line, we look at concern for people. Concern for people is rated on a scale of 1-9 with 1 being minimal concern for people and 9 being high concern for people. Concern for people is our leadership dimension of the grid. How involved with the people side of things do we need to be? What should we be looking at? We can break down concern for people into:

- Basic needs
- Safety
- Belonging and Love
- Esteem
- Self-actualization

We are looking at the needs of individuals within the organization. The same areas of needs that we look for in motivating employees are the areas we should focus our concern for people. If you are only worried about the team having enough income to survive, you are not overly concerned for people. If you are looking to support your team in self-actualization, you are highly concerned for people.

Higher scores on the Y-axis indicate a more leader-focused individual.

The original model defines five management styles based on scores with the grid:

1. Impoverished Management – Low People / Low Task
2. Country Club Management – High People / Low Task
3. Middle-of-the-Road Management – Mid People / Mid Task
4. Authority Compliance Management – Low People / High Task
5. Team Management – High People / High Task

Impoverished Management is a poor manager and a poor leader. When I think of impoverished management, I think of a fast-food restaurant that is filled with dirty tables, employees standing around talking at the counter while customers wait in line, and the bathroom is out of order. You cannot expect success in an environment where the manager or leader does not care about anything. Impoverished managers are often promoted to the role due to organizational need and availability. The manager may be selected because of tenure with the organization. Impoverished managers often do not want to be in the role but fill the role because they are required to.

Country Club Management is a poor manager but a good leader. The country club manager wants to take care of the team but is not concerned about the tasks. When looking for an example of country club management, it's in the name. When you think of a country club, the focus is far less on the quantity of customers that each employee can serve and much more focused on time spent with people. People pay a premium for country club membership, and the service is not about efficiency but availability. Country club managers are relationship and people-focused. They will protect their team and support their team, but they are not going to produce a high volume of tasks with their team.

Middle-of-the-Road Management is a balanced manager and leader. We can expect a lot of people to fall into this category. The middle-of-the-road manager is trying to balance the needs of the team with the needs of the organization. This is the manager who cares, but they aren't going to push everyone beyond their limits. The middle-of-the-road manager is probably happy in their position and generally feels balance in the work that they are completing.

Authority Compliance Management is a strong manager but a poor leader. When I spoke about my friend who joined my team, this is the leadership style that he grew up in. The authority compliance manager is only concerned with getting the task done. Personal issues do not matter when you are on the clock. Get the work done and be happy that you are getting paid. Authority compliance managers are singular in their focus, production. The manager will most likely be highly directive and offer little room for negotiation or compromise. Often, the leader does not care how the team perceives them. The leader cares about the work that needs to be done.

Team Management is the best of both worlds without any of the worst. Team managers are fully invested in their people and the work that they are completing. Team management is one of the most difficult types of management to achieve and to stay consistent in. Team management involves a high level of emotional investment and a high level of mental processing. When a manager is in team management, they are focused on the process side of management and the human side of leadership. When striving to improve as a leader, team management is the goal to strive for. Understand though, that not meeting the mark for team management is not the end of the world. There is always room for growth and improvement in our leadership. In most situations, I would recommend starting with a middle-of-the-road management style and slowly growing towards team management.

LEADERSHIP STYLES

Developing the leadership style that best suits you and your team will help you understand how you want to lead. When you look at the tools you have started to put into your toolbox, it is important to understand how you will access those tools and what the tools mean to the way that you lead.

Initially, it is important to understand that leadership styles are academic reference points that help people categorize and group leadership into different categories. People can make arguments about how a leader falls into one leadership category while someone else can paint a picture about the same leader falling into a different leadership category. Both can be correct.

Understanding the underlying characteristics of leadership styles is where the true value comes from in developing your own leadership style. You can look at different leadership styles and find what works for you and what you want to incorporate into your leadership style, or you may find things that do not work particularly well for you.

I plan to take you through seven leadership styles.

- Authentic Leadership
- Servant Leadership
- Transformational Leadership
- Transactional Leadership
- Democratic Leadership
- Authoritarian Leadership
- Laissez-Faire Leadership

AUTHENTIC LEADERSHIP

Authentic leadership is a leadership style that focuses on the leader's approach to leading his or her followers in a way that is innately tied to who the leader is as a person. Authentic leaders are truly genuine in their approach to leadership and personal citizenship. The leader does not assume a mask in filling the leadership role.

In many ways, it is easier to identify unauthenticity than to recognize authenticity. Think of a leader you know where the phrase "he's great when you get to know him away from work" applies. The leader is often strict and hard to work with, but in many ways is recognized as a great person away from work. The person assumes a mask when it is time to lead and drops the mask in other areas. This is not an authentic leader.

Authentic leaders are unabashedly true to who they are regardless of the situation. Authentic leaders place authenticity, transparency, and a focus on follower wellbeing at the forefront. The leadership style is typically accompanied by a strong ethical code. The authentic leader will not tolerate any deviations from their ethical code and will go out of their way to ensure that the code is followed.

When we look at authentic leadership as a leadership style, we are focusing on an internally focused leadership style. To be an authentic leader I need to be true to who I am as a person.

Developing authenticity in our leadership is not an easy feat. I used the example, "he's great when you get to know him away from work." Authentic leaders are the same at and away from work. When we are young in our leadership development, we often believe that we need to assume the role of leadership with a specific set of traits or qualities.

Historically, many leadership styles assumed that people were born as leaders, or all leaders had specific traits that needed to be emulated. We often assume that leaders are selected because they already demonstrate the required leadership traits. When we get put into that leadership role, we try to do the same thing. We assume what we think are leadership traits.

In developing authenticity in our leadership, we make the choice to lead the way we want to be led. We can focus on ensuring that the leadership that we practice matches our internal code of ethics. There are four key attributes to authentic leadership that highlight what it means to be authentic:

- Self-Awareness
- Self-Regulation
- Ethics
- Transparency

Self-Awareness should feel familiar. When we were looking at emotional intelligence as a tool in our toolbox, we started with being aware of our reactions. Self-Awareness is the inward-looking view of who you are as a person. What do you believe in? What drives you? What are you passionate about?

In a high paced world with a lot of distractions, it is easy to lose sight of what drives you individually. I have lost count of how many times I have come to an ice breaker activity and struggled to come up with a hobby I enjoy. I have four kids at home. My hobby is often getting them to the activities that they are involved with. That doesn't necessarily describe who I am though. I am a passionate father who enjoys quality time with my wife and children. I am motivated because I find passion in developing leaders. I want my children to see me passionate about what I do. I try to do things I am passionate about so that they learn authenticity in their passions as well. When I look inward, I can begin to see the connections between the different areas of who I am.

In my journey of self-evaluation, I had a role that stands out as a true example of leading with authenticity – I was developing

71

a project management office from the ground up. This has been a highlight of my career.

In that role, I made the conscious decision to connect with my team on a personal level. The door was opened so that they could share issues and concerns that they had in their personal lives. At the same time, I was transparent about what was happening in my own life. One vivid memory really captures the essence of authenticity in leadership; the PMP is a hallmark for project managers. Despite being eligible, I hadn't attempted the exam. Motivated by a desire to guide my team, I decided to take the exam. I took another training course, sat for the exam, and passed in less than a month. I wanted my team to see that it was achievable and send the message – if I can do it, so can you, and I'll be there to support you.

This commitment was put into action when one of my team members initiated the certification process under my leadership. It required me to prioritize my team, take a leap of faith, and confront my own anxieties. Throughout the journey, I remained open with my team about being nervous during the preparation for the challenging test, fostering an environment of shared vulnerability and growth.

Self-Regulation is a lot like our second step in emotional intelligence. Within self-regulation we ensure that we are in control of our actions. Authentic leaders self-regulate to ensure that what they do and say aligns with who they are and the ethical beliefs that they hold. An authentic leader does not want to have an outburst that is out of character. Outbursts that do not align with the general character of the leader would indicate a break in the consistent and present nature of the leader's authenticity.

Ethics are the framework that the leader uses to judge right from wrong. Ethics and morality are often used interchangeably, though it can be noted that ethics refers to the collective interpretation of values and morality refers to the individual code of right from wrong. When we look at authentic leaders, ethics is the need of the leader to shape the ethical engagement of the team, not only their perspective. The authentic leader is focused on creating an ethically sound environment for the success of the team and organization.

The code of ethics employed by the leader may not always align with the societal values of the time. Authentic leaders may pioneer new ethical values and norms that are not considered normal within the current time frame.

Transparency is our last key attribute for authentic leaders. Authentic leaders are clear in their messaging and do not hide their message as a secret code that needs to be deciphered. The leader wants followers to understand the message and the purpose of what they say. Authentic leaders provide transparency with honest and open communication.

A great example of an authentic leader is Vince Lombardi, the American football coach who led the Green Bay Packers from their worst season in 1959 to an impressive record in 1967. He is highly respected as a coach for his ability to turn the team from their worst season when he was appointed to the position to the end of his tenure with the team winning 105 games with 35 losses and 6 ties. He was often hated by his players because of his relentless methods. He expected greatness and would not compromise his expectations. He truly cared about his players though. He did not hide his values in order to pacify his players or the public. In a time where segregation was accepted as part of society, Vince Lombardi went out of his way to defy the segregationist practices with his team. He did not see black and white players; he saw a team of players. As a leader, he was passionate about his cause, leading the best players in the league. He did not worry about how people felt about him, he worried about pulling the best out of his players. While this did cause some of his players to hate him at the time, most have come to see him in high regard.

Authentic Leader Toolbox

Authentic leaders have similar toolboxes to other leaders. The tools that we discussed in the last section still apply. Emotional intelligence, empathy, motivation, and engagement are all tools at the disposal of the authentic leader. The way the leader uses the tool may vary from leader to leader based on the personality and the comforts of the leader, but all will be available to the leader. Because authentic leadership is an inward facing view of leadership, it does not dictate the way the leader engages with others.

Emotional Intelligence is an easily identifiable trait for authentic leaders. Facing inward, authentic leaders are aware of who they are and self-regulate to ensure that they stay consistent with who they are and who they want to be.

With sensitivity to their followers, most authentic leaders will understand **empathy**. The leader seeks transparency with communication. To ensure that communication is clear and presents an accurate representation of the leader's intentions, the leader needs to be able to actively listen to followers and not project their own thoughts into the perspective of followers.

The leader will find **motivation** techniques that align with personal beliefs. It is likely that an authentic leader will try to engage follower motivation at the belonging and love level, the esteem level, and work towards self-actualization. With a mission or cause focus, authentic leaders will build teams that support the mission or cause and begin working towards higher levels of motivation within the hierarchy of needs.

The authentic leader cares. Developing an **engagement** strategy for authentic leaders should drive a balance between the focus on task and people. The leader will be on the path between middle-of-the-road management to team management.

Authentic leadership is a great style of leadership to adopt, though it does require a level of comfort in one's own skin. The old adage "fake it until you make it" is not one you can adopt in authentic leadership. You need to always let your true colors fly and practice authenticity. You are good enough as you are. You will only get better as time moves forward.

SERVANT LEADERSHIP

Servant leadership flips the leadership paradigm upside down. The leader serves the followers. The leader places the needs and wellbeing of followers ahead of their own and allows followers to utilize their time, energy, and emotional capacity. The servant leader creates a connection with followers that extends beyond the work environment and creates a level of safety for the followers to discuss personal issues that are outside the scope of day-to-day interactions. Servant leaders are humble in their leadership. While they are in charge, they lead with humility and do not ask for benefits as a result of their position.

The connection that the leader establishes with followers does not require a friendship between the leader and the follower. The leader establishes a safe space where the follower is allowed to be vulnerable without fear of repercussion. Safety is created because the leader views the follower as a whole person who exists outside of the work environment.

I have always found the concept of servant leadership to be an intriguing type of leadership. The servant leader places the needs of the follower ahead of their own so that they can accomplish that task that supports the organization. By taking care of the people that follow me, they can better achieve the mission that I set before them.

Soldiers work long, hard hours and often are just getting their finances in order. When Soldiers have pay issues, which happens from time to time in the Army, it can bring that Soldier to an immediate halt. The Soldier has financial commitments that they need to be able to take care of. If they have a family, they need to ensure that their spouse and kids are taken care of. If they have a car or a house off post, they need to be able to take care of their expenses. An issue with pay will automatically reduce the effectiveness of the Soldier as they will be pulled away from the task at hand to focus on the hardship. As a servant leader, I can put myself in their shoes and it becomes my highest priority to take care of the Soldier. When the Soldier knows that they are in good hands and have the support they need, they can focus on the task at hand instead of the problem at hand.

History and religion provide a long list of servant leaders. When we look at the Judeo-Christian religions, we can see Moses as a servant leader. As a leader he led his people out of slavery, provided them with food and water, and gave them the ten commandments. Even when he learned at the end that he would not be able to enter the promised land, he continued to lead with humility and grace. When we look at Jesus as a Chrisitan example of servant leadership, we see the Son of God washing the feet of his disciples. He put the needs of his disciples and followers ahead of his own. He used the act of service as a lesson for his followers to practice servanthood and humility. In history we see figures like Martin Luther King, Jr. putting the needs of society ahead of his own safety. Despite the racial tension, he preached peace to achieve the dream of equality and the end of segregation.

While I personally regard servant leadership as a great style, there can be an unintended downside to servant leadership. Servant leadership can create an environment in which the organization feels emotional exhaustion. Servant leaders look for opportunities to give their time and energy to their followers. Followers who serve in the environment may begin to feel obligated to serve others in the same way. On the surface, this is positive. Beneath the surface, followers may emulate the behavior without feeling the commitment to the behavior. The followers will go through the motions without the internal commitment. If the internal commitment is lacking, the followers will worry more about keeping up an expected image than the actual acts of service.

Much like authentic leadership, servant leadership focuses inward on the leader's connection to leadership. The focus of how the leader serves followers is not prescriptive. The leader's interpretation is developmental to their interaction with followers.

Within servant leadership, four key attributes are:

- Ethics
- Personal Connection
- Communication
- Follower Empowerment

An **ethical** code is a large part of a servant leader's identity. Servant leaders are drawn to what they consider as right and moral. Servant leaders lead because at their core, the servant leader believes it is the right thing to do.

Servant leaders will develop an ethical code that is tied to their purpose. Many servant leaders have strong religious or cause focused convictions that drive their actions. The leaders will stay within their ethical boundaries because to do otherwise would be to neglect the followers who they serve.

Personal connection is a key driver for servant leaders. The servant looks to build a relationship with followers that extends beyond the workplace. If a follower has any problems, the servant leader is ready to assist. The mental, social, and economic success of followers directly impacts the ability of the follower to succeed. Building a connection involves establishing trust and living up to the expectation of availability. Many servant leaders will drop everything they are doing to take care of a follower who has an issue regardless of the time of day or what is going on.

To be an effective servant leader, you need to have availability in your day to respond to issues that arise. You need to be available to provide support. You can fill support time with activities that allow you to support and work with people in your team or in supporting teams.

In the Army, serving beside your followers is seen as the mark of a good leader. When Soldiers have a job that sucks like filling sandbags or digging a trench, it means a lot to them when you jump in the hole next to them and help them move the earth. As a leader, you are demonstrating that you are not above the work that you are asking them to do and that you care enough about them to spend time supporting them where they are working. It is not likely that you will move the earth any better than they will, but you are highlighting to those Soldiers that your place is beside them.

Communication is a critical attribute for servant leaders. Communication is how the servant leader lets people know about their purpose and their desire to support those who follow them. Communication allows the leader to establish personal connections with their followers.

Servant leaders look to communicate with clarity and transparency. Clarity is the ability to make sense of the message without additional input. It is important to the servant leader too because the servant leader does not want followers to waste time trying to decipher a message. A clear message empowers followers to act. Transparency is the level of work that followers need to exert to find the message. When I think of transparency, I often think about whether something is clear as water or clear as mud. Clear as water may have a different meaning if it is dirty pond water, but we can generally say if it's clear as water, we can see the full message from the beginning. If it is clear as mud, we have to dig for a message and we will be left wondering if there is anything else that we failed to find. In transparent communication, the leader ensures that nothing is hidden.

Follower Empowerment is the ability of the servant leader to allow followers to act. Servant leadership to a high degree begins with the leader removing obstacles to allow the followers to succeed. The leader begins from a place of servitude to ensure that followers do not have arbitrary obstacles placed in their way. Leaders use this starting point to enable followers to operate.

The second step for leaders is to empower action. Allow followers to make choices and decisions. The servant leader underwrites the decisions of followers and provides them with the backing that they need. When a follower makes a choice, it will not always be the right choice. The follower will make decisions that come with a cost. The leader though, is willing to assume the risk and provide the follower with the support necessary to come out of the decision in one piece. By empowering followers, there are greater opportunities to grow and succeed.

Servant Leader Toolbox

The toolbox for servant leaders is an inward focused toolbox. Servant leaders look for connection and the opportunity to provide help and support to their team. In order for the servant leader to lead, they must first find ways to serve their team. This sense of service creates an inward focus on how they can connect with others.

With a focus on connection, the servant leader begins with **Emotional Intelligence**. At a minimum, the servant leader is self-aware and possesses self-control. As a leader with a cause or purpose, there is a high level of self-awareness and self-control that are necessary for the leader. Most servant leaders will possess relationship awareness. The servant leader will be in tune with the reactions and perceptions of those around them. The leader will focus on the reactions to better serve the team. The final level of relationship management is likely a developed tool for the servant leader. The leader wants to meet the needs of followers. The ability of the leader to help shape and manage those needs will facilitate growth for the leader-follower relationship.

Empathy may be the strongest tool that the servant leader possesses. The servant leader is committed to listening. You cannot meet the needs of followers if you are not aware of their needs. In serving their followers, the leader validates their concerns. The needs of followers are valid and as a servant, the leader looks to honor those needs.

Servant leaders **motivate** from a Theory Y perspective. The servant leader operates from a perspective where they put the needs of others ahead of their own needs. This perspective lends to the thought that people generally want to achieve and need the right environment to succeed. When we put ourselves in a place of servitude, we look up to those we serve, not down on them. When it comes to motivation, the servant looks up to those they serve and sees them as people who are striving for the best.

The servant leader will help people rise through all of the levels within Maslow's Hierarchy. The leader will not resist a follower's higher-level needs from being met. The more successful the followers are, the more successful the servant leader feels.

There are three possible types of servant leaders when we look at **engagement**. The servant leader will be a country club manager, solely focused on the needs of followers even to the neglect of the task at hand, or they will balance people and task with middle-of-the-road management or team management. The servant leader will always have a high concern for people. The level of task focus will shift their effectiveness from a productivity perspective. The servant leader should always create an environment where people feel that they can succeed.

TRANSFORMATIONAL LEADERSHIP

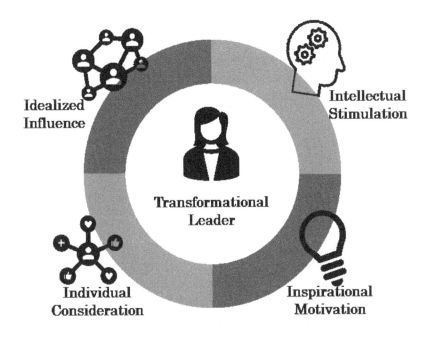

Transformational leadership is the process of inspiring people to change from within. The change transformational leaders seek is a positive change that supports the organization's direction. There are two key components that make the leader transformational; the leader needs to inspire, and followers need to connect with the change and internalize it. The transformational leader needs to move followers beyond their own self-interests and drive them to move as part of the greater organization.

The motivation a transformational leader inspires in people is internally focused and does not rely on transactions of this-for-that. The leader does not promise if you hit a metric, you will get a raise or promotion. The leader may promote you and give you a raise, but it is not a transaction it is goal achievement.

The difference between transformational and transactional leadership comes from the way the leadership is perceived by the followers. If the followers constantly need the transactions to continue in the direction the leader is heading, the leader has not achieved transformational leadership. If the leader does not need to conduct transactions because the followers understand and connect with the direction, the leader has become a transformational leader.

Leaders may slip in and out of transformational leadership. The leadership style is focused on the connection between the leader, the follower, and the purpose.

Historically, transformational leadership was tied to personality traits that a leader needed to possess to be a transformational leader. One of the key personality traits was charisma. When we think of leaders inspiring the masses, we envision a charismatic leader taking a stage and changing hearts and minds with a well-crafted speech. That really isn't the case though. Charisma may help a transformational leader, but the way the leader connects with followers is more important. There are four key attributes for transformational leaders.

- Intellectual Stimulation
- Inspirational Motivation
- Individual Consideration
- Idealized Influence

Intellectual Stimulation is the ability of the leader to challenge followers to think critically. The transformational leader challenges followers and team members to adopt change in a way that supports their role within the organization. That is hard to do if the leader is providing the answer to the follower without giving the follower the opportunity to solve the problem themselves.

The transformational leader is looking at the big picture and the way the team fits into the picture. The leader understands that allowing followers to develop their own solutions and tools will support a better process at the end of the change and a higher adoption rate from followers. The leader is not above the work but supports the process.

Inspirational Motivation is the way the leader develops a connection between followers and change. When we are children, our parents encourage us to eat new foods that we may not be interested in trying. They may bribe us. I know I have to bribe one of my kids. But parents will often say "try it, you might like it." The parent connects a desired result with a value that the child holds to motivate. The child wants to eat things that taste good. The parent wants the child to eat a diet with variety and nutrition. When the parent connects the motivation to the desires of the child, the change can be adopted more broadly in the future.

As leaders, inspiring motivation is more complex than getting your child to eat delicious Brussel sprouts. When a leader is looking to inspire change, the leader needs to connect the inspiration to the needs and desires of the follower. If a leader is interested in implementing reducing wasted time waiting, excessive time walking back and forth across a site, more steps than need to complete a task, or reduce the number of defects on a job, the leader may introduce lean principles on a jobsite, the leader needs to connect the change to a motivator the follower will connect with. Lean is a method for reducing waste in a process. Lean comes from the manufacturing world and looks to reduce waste in seven areas: transportation, inventory, motion, waiting, overproduction, overprocessing, and defects. Lean is a the process of making the job more efficient. How many foremen and supervisors have gotten upset because a laborer could not find a tool in the truck. Organizing the truck with labels supports the LEAN change. The leader can inspire motivation in the foreman by highlighting the reduced time laborers will spend searching for tools. The change is supported because the leader inspired motivation. The leader can tie it back to intellectual stimulation by supporting the foreman in finding the system that works best on that truck.

Individual Consideration is the way the leader focuses on each follower. Transformational leaders make each person feel valuable. Every member of the team matters to the transformational leader. Every member of the team has a role to play that supports the needs of the organization.

The transformational leader recognizes individual contributions and does not view the team as interchangeable cogs in a machine. Each team member supports a different aspect of the organization.

Utilizing the lean example, the leader would look for differences that multiple foremen offer for how to best organize their truck. Even though the leader may be looking to implement some standardization, the input from each foreman is valued. No one is left out of the standardization exercise and told to adopt what others have generated for them.

Our last attribute, **Idealized Influence** is how people view the leader. The leader serves as a role model. The leader adopts the same changes that is being requested of everyone. Idealized influence is built on authenticity. While not all authentic leaders are transformational, all transformational leaders are authentic leaders. The authenticity of the leader helps create the desire to follow. Idealized influence also speaks to the leader's ability to communicate vision and mission. Vision and mission let people know the desired goal and an idea of how to get there. It is hard to adopt a change without knowing the purpose behind the change.

What does transformational leadership actually look like?

One of the most famous cases of transformational leadership is Jack Welch. He was the eighth CEO of GE. When he took over the role of CEO, the organization was falling behind in the industry. The company was plagued with bureaucracy and redundancy. The internal management was not equipped to support the change and growth that the organization needed. Jack Welch focused on developing leadership within the organization and streamlining processes. GE regained a competitive advantage in the market and is still an industry leader. The Jack Welch Management Institute uses the lessons that he instilled in GE to train new leaders to this day.

While transformational leadership is generally considered a positive leadership style, it is often an aspirational style that may be difficult to maintain. The leadership style relies heavily on the personality and connections the leader makes to implement the changes within the organization. The direction of the organization will follow the path outlined by the leader. If the leader chooses a direction that is not inline with the current growth, the organization may begin to suffer from the poor decision with a high adoption rate. Transformational leaders are human and are subject to the same failings as their followers.

Transformational Leader Toolbox

Transformational leaders are authentic leaders and have the same starting point for their toolbox, but some of the tools will be focused on creating connections that drive change. Emotional intelligence, empathy, motivation, and engagement are all tools at the disposal of the authentic leader.

Emotional Intelligence is an easily identifiable trait for transformational leaders. The leaders are aware of who they are and self-regulate to ensure that they stay consistent with who they are and who they want to be. Emotional intelligence helps the leader create the connection necessary to motivate followers.

Individual consideration requires **empathy**. Each follower is unique and has a different set of needs. The leader needs to be able to actively listen to followers and not project their own thoughts into the perspective of followers.

87

The leader will find **motivation** techniques that align with the esteem level, and work towards self-actualization. Transformational leaders motivate from an internal perspective. Followers need to have their physiological, safety, and belonging/love needs met before the transformational leader can motivate at a transformational level.

The transformation leader drives an **engagement** strategy that balances the focus on task and people. The leader will be close to team management if they are not fully in the team management category.

Beginning as an authentic leader is the starting point to becoming a transformational leader. Transformational leaders find ways to engage and motivate their teams with an inner purpose that carries the organization forward. Transformational leaders emerge in times of change. The leadership style requires the organization to change around the leader. With this in mind, you can create an impact on your organization without changing it. By changing the organization, you will shape the way the organization conducts business in the future.

TRANSACTIONAL LEADERSHIP

Transactional leadership is a managerial style of leadership that focuses on what followers will earn for tasks completed. As the name implies, transactional leadership focuses on transactions between the leader and the follower. Transactional leaders agree to specific rewards in exchange for follower participation.

There is often debate that is fueled by perception to indicate whether a leader is transformational or transactional. As we discussed in the last section, transformational leaders create an internal inspiration that drives the follower. Transactional leaders create external motivation. While the transformational leader may provide rewards for completing a task, the rewards add to the intrinsic satisfaction of completing the task. Transactional leaders must provide an external reward, such as a raise, bonus, time off, or similar motivation to gain traction in completing a task out of the ordinary. From the transactional and transformational leaders' perspective, they may be operating in the same way. The perception of followers is where the distinction between the two truly takes place. The transactional leader does not create the same inspirational motivation or intellectual stimulation.

Henry Ford is often credited with being a very successful transactional leader. Henry Ford founded the Ford Motor Company and is credited for the success of the assembly line. He was an incredibly intelligent leader who found ways to motivate employees, but it can be said that he did not create a personal connection with the work force. He was the leader and if they wanted to earn a living in his company, they were welcome to work. He improved working conditions for employees to attract new employees. His goal was not to inspire, but to attract.

Henry Ford introduced the $5 day. Employees were paid a higher salary to encourage employees to work for him and to produce at a higher rate. $5 per day was nearly double the current wage at the time. Employees would meet higher productivity rates because they wanted to stay employed at Ford Motor Company. They would not be able to earn the same wages outside of the company. The wage is a tangible reward employees can earn for the work that does not create an internal desire to complete the work.

Simplicity was another tool that Henry Ford introduced in order to increase efficiency in his production line. At the time, skilled craftsmen would complete large portions of the automobile utilizing their skill and time to move through the process. The assembly line broke down the skilled process into small repetitive tasks. Employees could be employed with little to no skill to complete tasks that historically required a high level of skill. Employees could now be rewarded for completing tasks quickly and accurately.

Ford Motor Company was also known for strict rules and regulations. The rules and regulations governed employee dress code and personal hygiene. Failure to comply with the rules and regulations had negative consequences. Employees were encouraged to follow the rules and regulations because the trade off meant losing an irreplaceable wage for the time.

Transactional leadership focuses on creating a system for rewards and consequences. The transactional leader does not typically choose the transactional leadership style and often does not recognize that they are transactionally focused. The transactional leadership style is often a default style for individuals who are looking for ways to motivate others.

There a few key attributes for transactional leaders:

- Rewards and Punishments as Motivation
- Focus on Tasks and Objectives

- Short-term Focus
- Directive Communication
- Performance Management Focus

Transactional leaders implement a structure that utilizes **rewards and punishments as motivation**. The leader will establish an environment that identifies what is and is not acceptable. Followers are expected to meet the requirements or leave the organization.

A **focus on tasks and objectives** is critical to the transactional leader. The transactional leader is outcomes based. The leader is investing resources to achieve a specific outcome. The rewards and punishments the leader develops are to create an environment where tasks and objectives can be completed.

Transactional leaders typically have a **short-term focus** and do not create long-term plans. This is truer in junior leadership than it is senior leadership. Henry Ford is the exception to this rule, not the rule. With a constant focus on tasks and objectives, rules and compliance, and day-to-day, it is difficult for the transactional leader to look long-term. The minutia that the leaders focus on requires energy that is pulled from other areas. Long-term planning requires more energy to bring into focus.

Directive communication is common with transactional leaders. Transactional leaders are focused on managing the process and ensuring that needed incentives are in place. They are not looking to build a relationship with their team. As a result, communication is often direct and to the point. The leader will give the directions that are necessary but does not seek dialogue in return. Directive communication pairs well with the focus on tasks and the short term. Directive communication facilitates tasks that do not require creativity or independent processing. Because directive communication creates one sided conversation, the communication does not support long-term objectives. The leader is not positioned to receive feedback from team members.

Our last attribute is a **performance management focus**. Transactional leaders look for team members who operate within the rules and regulations that have been established. Performance management is a method for identifying and rewarding team members who perform well within the rules and regulations that have been established. Performance management allows the leader to lean heavily into the rewards and punishments that are used to encourage motivation.

Overall, transactional leadership is not a very personal leadership style. It relies on management over leadership and often fails to intrinsically motivate a team. It does have the positive aspect of establishing a framework where expectations are clear and team members understand what is required for advancement. The leadership style is responsible for the success of the Ford Motor Company. In environments where creativity and independent thought are not a requirement, transactional leadership may be a successful option.

Transactional Leadership Toolbox

The transactional leadership toolbox relies far less on emotional intelligence and empathy than our previous leadership styles. Transactional leadership is less of a leadership style and more of a management style. The focus is less on creating bonds that inspire and more on creating incentives that people are willing to work for.

The transactional leader may have **emotional intelligence** at the self-awareness or self-control level, but it is unlikely that the transactional leader is concerned with relationship awareness or relationship management. Emotional intelligence as a tool does not align with the leader's perspective. Emotions and feelings are not a commodity that can be leveraged for increasing productivity. The transactional leader is more likely to offer a pizza party to reward success than to look at ways to influence followers with personal connection.

Empathy is an area where a transactional leader is likely to struggle. The first step in empathy is to actively listen with the second step being to validate the other person. Transactional leaders look at engagements as part of a business dealing where empathy does not support the transaction. The leader often has ideas in place for how the work should be executed. The leader is not likely to listen to someone else's ideas and is equally unlikely to validate the ideas.

Transactional leaders will lean towards a Theory X philosophy of employees in **motivation** strategies. The leader is concerned with finding the right incentives that will encourage followers to work. Everything is based on compensation with little to no thought of internal motivation. The leader will focus on lower levels of needs in Maslow's Hierarchy. The leader will ensure that the follower has physiological needs and safety/security needs met but will not put much effort into love and belonging, self-esteem, or actualization. The higher order needs do not align with transactions. The leader can compensate followers with a salary, benefits, and other needs that meet physical and safety requirements. A sense of family and connection is not tradeable. The leader cannot offer connection when everything is a transaction.

When looking at **engagement,** the transactional leader is highly focused on the task. The leader wants to ensure that the task is completed. Focus on the people will be lower for the leader. People focus is ancillary to the task. The leader may look at ways to motivate people to achieve a higher output of tasks, but the focus will be secondary. The leader will most likely fall into authority compliance management but may stray towards middle-of-the-road management.

Transactional leadership is not one of my favorite leadership styles and can easily come across as a negative leadership style. The positive components of transactional leadership is that it provides solid structure and consistency. For followers who personally align with Theory X, the leadership style provides a framework where they are able to succeed. As a leader, I find that I am drawn to more personal styles of leadership and follower empowerment, but there is a case for leadership styles that hold people at a greater distance.

DEMOCRATIC LEADERSHIP

Democratic leadership is a leadership style that promotes the ability of followers to vote on an outcome when decisions are required. A truly democratic leadership style would allow the full team to have an equal vote or participation in decision making. In reality, democratic leaders gather opinions or votes from their team and render a decision based on the opinions.

To be truly democratic would require leaders to consistently act as a moderator in identifying decision points and bringing the decisions before the team for a decision. The team would have the opportunity to decide as a group on each decision and present their rational for the decision to the group.

In a practical sense, the democratic leader retains the leadership role and holds decision making authority. The leader gathers and weighs input from the team to ensure that the team believes in the decision that the leader is making.

An environment where all voices are entirely equal and there is not a singular decision maker is an environment that will become mired in indecision. Even partnerships with two decision makers require structure to break differences of opinion.

Democratic leadership in practice can take on different shapes and forms that involve soliciting input from team members to ensure that the team supports the decision-making process. Democratic leaders are focused on bringing together the thoughts of the group and soliciting input. Democratic leaders maintain balance and often foster environments that support a high level of communication across the team.

Leaders will often pull together specialized groups to support the decision-making process. The groups represent teams across the organization with specific skill sets. The leader looks to incorporate knowledgeable input from the different respective areas across the organization. When the leader is satisfied that the decision is well rounded with the support of the organization, the leader will sign off on the decision.

When I think about democracy and democratic leadership, I often think about ancient Greece and Rome where the citizens had a vote in the development of law. Scholars would debate each other to ensure that decisions were made with facts and not based solely on opinion. Democracy is a romantic concept that promotes equality and representation.

I want to highlight, when we look at democratic leadership it is easy to jump to the government as the idea of democracy. Our government has fought wars over democracy. We have fought for the right of representation. When we discuss democratic leadership in this context, we are looking at the leadership style without the governmental context. We are looking at the leadership style in a smaller context.

Early in my Army career, I was a platoon leader for 32 Soldiers. I had recently graduated from college and participated in the initial training the Army provides to new lieutenants. I had Soldiers who I was responsible for leading who had more experience in the Army and in the tasks that we were completing. I had the least time in service compared to many. Much of my platoon had recently come back from a combat deployment.

Leading the Soldiers in my platoon often felt difficult because my rank and position put me in charge, but I had to balance my position with their knowledge and expertise.

Democratic leadership was a way for me to build a relationship that incorporated their knowledge into the plans and orders I was responsible for producing. I maintained my responsibility, but I was able to leverage input from people with a lot more experience than what I possessed. I could ask for input and support without giving up my authority.

When we began running training missions, I would leverage the leaders in my platoon to provide input and insight into the best methods for planning missions. Early input from my leaders also created buy-in from the leaders in the decisions that were made. It also eased the burden of issuing orders because my leaders were already aware of the part their element would play when the mission brief was given.

It was not always easy. I had a lot of leadership turnover while I was a platoon leader. Acting as a democratic leader helped me develop an understanding of my leaders' strengths.

As a new leader, serving as a democratic leader was the right choice for me. I could bring people into the decision-making process and build buy-in from the team.

I have been in leadership roles since the platoon leader role where a democratic approach was less appropriate. I imagine a lot of platoon leaders would not have found the democratic approach to be successful. For me it worked because I could bring the right people in at the right time.

Democratic leadership focuses on the relationship between the leader and followers in decision-making. The leadership style can be clearly evaluated from outside the team. Democratic leaders can be spotted based on the way they interact with their teams and followers.

There are 5 key attributes to democratic leaders:

- Commitment to Participation
- Transparent Communication
- Collaboration
- Interpersonal Skills
- Ethics

Democratic leaders are **committed to participation** from their team. The leader ensures that the team has the opportunity to get involved with the decision-making process and be a part of the solution. The leader is driven to ensure that people are heard. Every election cycle, there are people who set up booths and hand out flyers encouraging people to vote. While many of them are focused on a single candidate or party, there are others who are out to support the democratic spirit of the election process. Democratic leaders have the same passion for the process.

Transparent communication has been a common theme in leadership styles that create a personal connection between the leader and the follower. Transparent communication creates trust and purpose within the relationship. Democratic leaders favor transparent communication because it allows followers to make informed decisions. Without transparent communication followers would make uninformed decisions that may not have the intended effect.

Democratic leaders place a high value on **collaboration**. Collaboration is an effect of participation and communication meeting to bring people together on a topic. Collaboration can take on different shapes and sizes within a team. The process can look like followers involved in the planning process. It can take the shape of work groups that are focused on solving a particular problem. Collaboration may look like a room with a team brainstorming ideas for the next project they will work on. In a construction setting, it may be the office sending a potential design to the team who will build it prior to finalizing the design.

Interpersonal skills are necessary to foster communication and collaboration. If you want everyone to contribute and participate, you need to know how to interact with them. Interpersonal skills are layered in our tools from the toolbox.

Our last attribute is **ethics**. Similar to transparent communication, leaders who create a personal connection with followers have ethics that shape the way they behave. For democratic leaders, an ethical foundation promotes equality and voice within the operation of the team. It is hard to want everyone to have a voice and be heard if you don't believe that everyone is equal. That belief in equality is the foundation of ethics.

Democratic Leadership Toolbox

The tools in the democratic leadership toolbox are very centered on fostering communication within a team. High emotional intelligence and empathy are used to ensure that the team feels that they are able to contribute to team decision making.

Emotional Intelligence is a common focus for democratic leaders. The leader will possess self-awareness and self-control and should have at least a basic understanding of relationship awareness. Leaders who spend a long time as democratic leaders will begin to develop a strong sense of relationship management. Higher levels of emotional intelligence help the leader motivate the team in the decision-making process and gain support for changes and improvements.

Empathy is important to the democratic leader. The leader should be specifically tuned in to listening. In finding ways to bring the team towards common goals and objectives, the leader will be interested in where the team currently identifies. The leader should focus on what team members are saying and how they are motivated or demotivated by the decision-making process. Validation should come easy for the democratic leader. The leader is interested in finding solutions that are fully supported by the team. Invalidating a perspective would diminish the trust the leader is working to build. Not projecting or casting judgement may not be as natural as the skills take time to develop, but the leader will look to ensure that the team can trust in the decision-making process.

Motivation will lean towards a Theory Y perspective that all individuals within the team want to contribute. The leader needs to ensure that base level needs are met but can focus on higher order needs. The democratic leader wants people to have a sense of love and belonging and will work on developing self-esteem. The democratic leader motivates by acknowledging and promoting positive contributions to the team. As democratic leaders spend more time with their teams, they can work towards self-actualization. The leader will begin letting the team lead initiatives that support growth.

Engagement will lean towards a people focus. The leader wants the team to be engaged and happy with the decisions that need to be made. Some democratic leaders may struggle to balance people focus with a task focus. Other democratic leaders will walk the balance effectively by pulling the team focus to productivity. On the managerial grid, the leader is likely to fall between the country club management and middle-of-the-road management. More developed democratic leaders will be able to manage in the team management area. Personality will play a large role in the leader's engagement style. The way the leader pulls the team's focus to the task in decision-making will be the deciding factor.

Democratic leadership is a sound leadership style that is great for taking input from across a team. The leadership style can have a propensity to take longer to make decisions. Some democratic leaders may lose a sense of ownership over decisions and give up their authority to the team. This can create situations where decisions are not made to avoid crisis or get out of a crisis situation. Used within limits that maintain accountability and authority, democratic leadership is a strong leadership style. I personally leaned on the style when I led smaller teams with greater expertise than I possessed.

AUTHORITARIAN LEADERSHIP

Authoritarian leadership is one of the most recognizable yet frequently criticized leadership styles. Authoritarian leadership is a leadership style that identifies the leader as the singular decision-maker who holds authority over the team. The authoritarian leader does not have followers. The authoritarian leader has employees, subjects, or subordinates. People don't often choose to work under an authoritarian leader but may stay depending on their personality type.

The leader does not look for input from team members as we see in democratic leadership. The leader isn't looking for ways to connect with the people on the team. The leader is considered the expert in the process.

Subject matter expertise is often why authoritarian leaders are selected to lead. In trades, the guy who is best at the job often gets promoted to a position of leadership. For someone not inclined to personal leadership styles, authoritarian leadership becomes the default.

"You will do as you are told, I am in charge."

The approach works in areas where creativity and problem solving are not required of those on the team. The style does not build a team that is intent on staying with the team. It may create future experts who will become leaders, but it does not create a sense of loyalty to the leader or the team.

With authoritarian leadership, the team becomes an extension of the leader. The leader uses a team member to accomplish a specific task. On a rough framing construction crew, an authoritarian foreman may divvy up the tasks where the foreman reads the prints and marks the layout of the wall to be built; one team member will focus be designated as the cut-man; another team member will run lumber across the site, and the last team member is nailing everything in as the foreman laid it

101

out. Only one person is really being asked to think, process, and solve problems: the leader. The leader flexes the team where needed. When it is time to stand the wall up, the leader reallocates people to pull everyone to the singular point needed and then sends them to the next position.

Some leaders are highly effective using authority alone to get things done, but the style does not allow for input from others to think critically. People are required to do what they are told, when they are told, and they are not expected to question it.

Authoritarian leadership is how dictators lead. When we look at dictators, we see a singular point of power that is often corrupt. Dictators do not make people say I want to be just like that guy. People fight against dictators.

In the beginning of the book, I talked about Jay who worked for me that experienced authoritarian leadership working for his dad and laissez-faire leadership in the role prior to working for me. On a crew, his dad expected 100% compliance with what he said. There was no room for arguing. There was no room for suggestion. Jay's dad was incredibly smart and dedicated to the work. He showed up early to plan the work and knew what needed to be done and when it needed to be done. Arguing with him undermined the work that he had already done. He didn't have time to waste worrying about telling you to get things done the "right" way. He would not avoid saying anything that could hurt your feelings. Feelings did not have a place on the jobsite. You could worry about your feelings later, after the workday.

I had the opportunity to work with his dad. He ran a very tight jobsite and consistently made the company money. When I worked with him, he had mellowed out with age, but he was focused on the process and the order behind the work taking place. His authority in his position was derived from his knowledge of his trade. Years of experience qualified him for the role that he was in.

Authoritarian leadership can be seen from an outside perspective. The focus is on the interaction between the leader and the subordinate.

There are three key attributes to authoritarian leadership:

- Dominance and Control
- Assertiveness
- Limited consideration of others

Dominance and control are where the leader exerts power over the full team with a position of highest authority. The leader is going to make all of the decisions and expects the team to align with the decisions made. The leader focuses on their own judgement and expertise. The leader will share what is necessary for work accomplishment but will not provide more communication than is necessary.

The leader's independent control over the team allows for **assertiveness** in decision-making. The leader is not going to consult the team for support in the decision-making process. Unlike the democratic leader, who can become mired in the decision-making process, the authoritarian leader is capable of making a decision on the spot and sticking to it. The leader has visions and goals for where the team is going and how the team will get there. The vision and goals are limited by the leader's own span of control and are typically focused on tangible ideas. Within the leader's assertiveness, the leader becomes an effective communicator. The leader expects full compliance with direction, the team cannot complete exacting tasks without clear direction.

Limited consideration of others is what makes most teams dislike their authoritarian leader. The leader has a vision and a goal. The team has specific functions to accomplish. If the team is not able to accomplish their task, regardless of reason, the leader is hindered from completing the goal. While the leader may occasionally compromise with the team members, it is an exception and not the rule. The leader typically lacks emotional intelligence and empathy. Some, certainly not all, authoritarian leaders will use intimidation as a tool to get the job done. The team will do as they are told or there will be consequences. Similar to transactional leaders who use rewards and punishments, the authoritarian leader will use punishments when they deem it necessary. Some authoritarian leaders can become corrupt within their organization.

We typically do not have a lot of good things to say about authoritarian leaders, but it is still a default leadership style for many leaders. It is simplistic as there is no question of control. The simplicity limits the effectiveness of the style in roles that require creativity and independent thought. When we discussed leadership capital earlier in the book, authoritarian leaders burn through leadership capital faster than they replenish it. The leader will see turnover that is abrupt and often comes with little notice. Employees will finally have enough and walk out. There is a harder breaking point that causes a departure than what other leaders experience. Some authoritarian leaders use the leadership style as a mask that is dropped after the work concludes. The dropping of the mask brings out their true personality. This break may allow some employees to tolerate the leader on the jobsite because they like the other side of the boss.

Authoritarian Leadership Toolbox

There are not a whole lot of tools in the authoritarian leader's toolbox. The leader does not use emotional intelligence or empathy which limits the way the leader can use motivation and engagement.

Emotional Intelligence is an absent tool because it is overridden by the limited consideration of others. The leader may have self-awareness to the extent that the leader can recognize pet peeves and things that put them in a good mood. The leader is less likely to have self-control. The leader will see emotions as influenced by the people led. The leader will not take accountability for their own emotions. The leader does not worry about relationship awareness or relationship management. The leader is not at work to coddle feelings. The leader is at work to get a job done.

Empathy would be difficult to find on a jobsite run by an authoritarian leader. The leader is not willing to listen, they will not be open to active listening. The leader does not need to validate a perspective they are unwilling to listen to. The leader is not concerned about projecting their perspective. The leader will give direction and a limited amount of advice, but it is entirely from the experience and perspective of the leader. The leader will judge what the team member is going through. There is no incentive or rationale for the leader not to judge. The perspective of "don't put yourself in stupid situations if you don't want stupid consequences" is the more likely perspective of the leader.

The leader will approach **motivation** from a Theory X perspective. People need to be directed to do everything because they are inherently lazy and are not concerned about getting the job done without being told when and how to work. The leader will ensure that the team members have basic physiological needs met but will only offer limited safety needs. The leader will ensure that the team has a place to stay, food, water, and proper gear to stay warm or cool. The leader will ensure safety procedures are followed to prevent injury on the jobsite. The leader does not often create a sense of security. Employees are replaceable. If an employee does not do what is expected, they can expect to be sent home. The lack of security often motivates compliance before the breaking point.

The authoritarian leader uses an **engagement** strategy that has a high task focus and a low people focus. Most authoritarian leaders use an authority compliance management style. It is in the name. Do what is expected and everything will be fine. Fight the system and see the results.

105

The limited number of tools in the authoritarian leader's toolbox makes it hard for the leader to maintain a team long term. The leader will experience high turnover within the team. People will find the leadership capital account empty and find a new place to work. People who are newer to the trade may do well under the leadership style though as they have the opportunity to learn from someone who is experienced and skilled.

LAISSEZ-FAIRE LEADERSHIP

The last leadership style we will explore is laissez-faire leadership. I purposely set this style as the last style we discussed and sequenced democratic, authoritarian, and then laissez-faire leadership. In scholarly writings, the three styles are often compared on a spectrum of control. Democratic leaders are extremely collaborative. Authoritarian leaders are extremely controlling. Laissez-faire leaders are very hands off.

The term laissez-faire originates from the French term "laisser faire" which mean "let them do".

Laissez-faire leaders let their teams do what they need to do. The leader does not interject control into the relationship with followers. The hands-off nature of the leadership style essentially makes the leadership style an oxymoron. Leading is the act of inspiring others to do things they would not do on their own. Laissez-faire leaders allow their team to operate without guidance or interference from the leader. It is hard to reconcile laissez-faire leadership as a true leadership style. It is more of a management philosophy that allows a well-functioning team to continue functioning.

While the leadership style is hands off, it can be an effective style in an environment that has high performers that know what needs to be done and when it needs to be done. Self-motivated followers will perform well under a laissez-faire leader, but employees without ambition will not have the direction necessary to flourish in the environment. Leaders need to challenge their followers and provide opportunities for growth. While laissez-faire leaders may have high performers, it is unlikely that the followers are challenged to step out of their comfort zone. They will operate where they are comfortable because it is what makes them comfortable.

In practice, Jay and I worked with a laissez-faire leader. Jay worked for a leader who was predominately a laissez-faire leader before he came to work for me. His laissez-faire leader allowed him the freedom to define the way his work tasks were completed and allowed him flexibility in his approach as long as the needs of the organization were met. He was able to define and develop the shape of his role because he was not pressured by his boss to operate in a specific way.

The downside was that he often felt that he had to figure things out without support from his leadership. The work that he was doing did not always have a clearly defined focus or timeline. The situation created issues when it came to deadlines for projects that he was not aware of. He would find himself in a crunch to meet a deadline he did not realize was approaching because he was not aware of an agreement that took place outside of the office.

He became adept at self-development during his time in the role, but he lacked formal professional development.

From a leadership standpoint, laissez-faire leadership is lacking. It does not inspire followers, it does not develop followers, and it does not create an environment of growth. From a management perspective, laissez faire leadership has the potential to be effective. High performers who do not require constant guidance and feedback can perform well under a laissez-faire leader. The follower does not need to worry about micromanagement or critical reviews. The follower is allowed to shape and guide the nature of the work.

Laissez-faire leadership focuses on the interaction between the leader and the follower. The follower's perception of leader engagement is the mark of whether or not a leader is a laissez-faire leader.

Laissez-faire leadership has four key attributes:

- Delegation
- Minimal Intervention
- Low Control

- Comfort with Ambiguity

The laissez-faire leader will **delegate** tasks and decisions down to their followers. Delegation allows followers to take ownership of the tasks they are assigned and define the method and approach that they take to satisfying the requirement. The leader is less concerned with the approach the follower takes and is more concerned that the task is accomplished. Delegating tasks removes the leader from the process. Delegating is neutral in the sense of good or bad. Delegating a task to a strong team has the potential to be great. Delegating to a poor team can be bad. The skills and ethics of the team decide whether delegation is positive or negative.

Minimal intervention is the trademark of laissez-faire. Let it be. Sometimes minimal intervention is the key to success. A strong capable team does not need a leader trying to make decisions in an environment where the experts are hard at work. The leader can slow a process that is running effectively. Minimal intervention can also create problems that require far more energy and resources to correct than an early intervention. I led a program where my boss was fairly hands off in the beginning. He was not going to interfere. When I recognized issues and asked for help, he still did not interfere. The contract went sideways, and we could not throw enough resources into the program at the end to make it profitable. Intervention from my boss would have helped me in the situation.

When I think about minimal intervention, I think of the saying "it is better to keep your mouth shut and be thought a fool than to open your mouth and prove it." Leaders can serve their teams by not intervening when the team has everything under control. Leaders can lose their teams by not intervening when the team needs support.

Laissez-faire leaders keep a **low control** environment. The leader grants freedom and flexibility with how tasks are accomplished. The low control creates an environment that allows creative people to really grow. Followers do not need to ask permission before asking and often feel the comfort of taking risks that they would not be comfortable with in other leadership styles.

The laissez-faire leader is **comfortable with ambiguity** and expects the team to be comfortable as well. The leader does not need the details of how a team will solve a problem. The leader will often allow the team to develop the approach that works for them.

Overall, laissez-faire leadership has its strengths and weaknesses. It is much better suited to some teams than others.

Laissez-Faire Leadership Toolbox

The leadership toolbox for a laissez-faire leader looks different for each laissez-faire leader and will vary from team to team that they lead. The hands-off approach to laissez-faire leaders minimizes the need for emotional intelligence and empathy. The leader allows work to progress without interference but is not engaged in developing the team to succeed. The leader does not need to place a lot of time into the interpersonal relationship.

It is really hard to say a laissez-faire leader will be at any level of **emotional intelligence**. The leader may be hands off because they don't deal well with emotional intelligence, or they may be hands off because they want to give their followers the opportunity to develop, and they know they can successfully manage the relationship by creating a hands-off environment that allows the follower the opportunity to be creative.

Empathy is a strong maybe in a laissez-faire leader. The leader may be available if the follower needs them, or the leader may not want the details that impact how the follower is feeling. Without understanding the nature of why the leader has chosen a laissez-faire leadership style, it is hard to understand how much empathy they have.

Laissez-faire leaders will view **motivation** from a neutral standpoint on whether they believe followers are self-motivated or they will believe in Theory Y, that people inherently want to do good things for the organization. The leader allows people space to show whether they are internally motivated or not. The leader's motivation, whether apathetic or invested, is an indication of where their beliefs lie. The leader will most likely ensure that systems are in place to provide for physiological needs and safety needs. A truly laissez-faire leader is not as concerned with needs for love and belonging. The leader wants the work to be done but is separated from the environment.

The leader will view **engagement** with little thought for people and slightly more for the task. The leader will typically fall between impoverished management and authority compliance management. The leader wants the task completed but does not want to be involved in the process. The leader is unlikely to yell or get upset with the followers, which pulls them back from the authority compliance management level, but the lack of personal engagement limits the people focus of the leader.

We have explored seven leadership styles. Leadership styles are all singular definitions of leadership that can be taken to develop a holistic style of leadership. You are not limited to any one singular style of leadership. You can fluctuate through multiple leadership styles depending on the situation you find yourself in.

Your leadership style will shift and change as you develop. That is great. Embrace it. Try new things.

We started off talking about authentic leadership because I think it is important to decide whether your leadership style is who you are or something you step into for a role. There have been times in my career that I have put on a leader mask that was not authentic. There have been times in my career that I could be myself in and out of the role. I could distance myself from the role when it was a mask, but I felt more comfortable when I could truly be authentic. Part of the difference was my comfort in leading.

As you develop your leadership style, you can try out as many leadership styles as your followers have the patience for.

We wrapped up with democratic, authoritarian, and laissez-faire leadership. Each style has different strengths and weaknesses. You can use a blend of the three styles, developing an environment where your team knows that you have their back and value their opinions but also that you will make the final decision when it is required. You can then take a step back and allow the team to operate when it is operating well.

Leadership requires a lot of balancing. We balance the tasks that we need to meet. We balance the needs of our team. We balance our needs within the team. We balance the needs of our family and friends who are supporting us from the sidelines.

I hope that as you read through the different leadership styles you found things that you both like and dislike. You can use multiple leadership styles to craft the style that best suits you. Nothing says you can't be an authentic transformational democratic leader. You can be a transformational servant leader. You can be hard to define.

Theories are great for helping us put words to what it is we are seeing. Theories help us rationalize the why and create connections between what we are seeing and experiencing. Theories suck at actually helping us create the effect we are looking for. We are still responsible for making it happen.

Reflection Questions

1. Is there a particular leadership style that you think you currently fall into?
2. Is there a leadership style that you would like to move towards?
3. Do you think it's fine to shift between styles?
4. When you think about the different styles, do you think you can apply different styles to different team members?
5. Can you find a leader you know to match each style?
6. Is there a leadership style you definitely want to stay away from?
7. Is there a leadership style you want to learn more about?
8. Do you think leaders should be close with their team or have a healthy distance?
9. Do you think one style of leadership gets more respect than others?
10. Do you have the tools to be the type of leader you want to be?

COACHING

We started off with four basic tools in our toolbox. We have emotional intelligence, empathy, motivation, and engagement. We can use all of those tools to lead a team. Coaching is a tool that we can add to our toolbox to make our teams more successful with long-lasting results. Coaching is an investment in each team member that pays for the time spent on future performance. Coaching can take on a different look with each leader-team member dynamic.

As leaders, we have teams of individuals who will encounter situations where some plays will work better than others. We need to empower our team members by helping them develop tools that will help them in a future situation.

When you take on the role of coach, you need to take a step back from any problems that may be a focal point for your team members. Your goal is not to solve the problem but to help them identify a solution to the problem. You can help guide them to the solution, but you cannot just give them the answer.

Coaching is most often associated with sports. Every team has a coach or a team of coaches who develop the skills of the players on the field so that they can perform when the game time comes. During practice, the coach is on the field, giving guidance, correcting errors, and looking for ways to hone players' skills. During the game, the coach is on the sideline. The coach may tell the team what play will work, but it is the responsibility of the team captain to implement the play on the field. The team captain has the option to ignore the coach and run a different play. The team captain is leading the team on the field. The coach is on the sideline. The trust and respect the team captain has will affect whether the coach's play or a different play is used on the field.

Learning to coach often requires the focus to shift the mindset. Remember, many leaders are selected because they are good at what they do. They are problem solvers. They solve a lot of problems.

That's not what you need to do in a coaching situation.

When I think about coaching, I often think about the early parts of my military career when I did not know how to coach and compare it to more recent parts of my career, where coaching has become a natural part of my leadership style.

One memory that stands out to me as a failure to coach is when I was a new platoon leader. I had only been in the role for a few months. My company commander identified two issues with one of my soldiers, SGT L, related to the soldiers' finances. SGT is short for sergeant. The first issue was that SGT L had a government-issued travel card, which is a credit card that often serves as a nightmare for soldiers and leaders. It had not been paid off after travel from before I had even arrived at the unit. Not paying the government travel card is a huge issue. It hurts his credit number one, but it also is a reportable metric that is seen by senior leadership. His was on the AGED report, which made it a problem that went up several levels. The second issue was more unique to the military. SGT L also had a geographically separated spouse, but he was not providing her with financial support. She was working in a position where she did not need support. Living apart was due to where the Soldier was stationed being away from where his wife lived. When they had issues, she would let the company commander know that he was not supporting her. When they resolved the issues, she would tell him not to worry about providing support. This would have been a great opportunity for coaching.

That's not what I did. I brought up the issues with him for the first time to let SGT L know the issues existed. I did not ask for a specific resolution, but I did let him know that it needed to be taken care of. I was working at being a democratic leader. I wanted him to buy into the solution, but I also didn't want to create an uncomfortable situation.

115

The next month, both issues raised their heads again, and I was directed to have a more deliberate conversation with SGT L. I looked into possible resolutions, and I tried to approach the situation with answers in hand. The problem was that SGT L did not agree that these were problems that needed to be solved. He viewed the government travel card as a government problem. He had not received the money to pay for the card, and he did not want to pay out of pocket. If he got the money, which he should have gotten, he would pay the card off. There was a broken process, but he wasn't interested. In the second issue, SGT L did not see a need to provide support when she specifically told him not to worry about it. He felt his relationship was his business, and the Army did not need to have a say in things.

It got a little heated. Rather than coach to a solution, I tried on an authoritarian leadership style. I neglected emotional intelligence. I abandoned empathy. I didn't worry about his sense of safety or sense of belonging, and financial insecurity can cause issues with safety. I told him he would fix the issues. I gave him directions on fixing the issues with the government travel card. I gave him a few options on how to handle the spouse issue.

I didn't coach.

It hurt the relationship between the two of us, which had never been great. SGT L left the unit and was stationed at a different base shortly after this engagement. To this day, I think about that conversation as a missed opportunity. It could have been a much better situation if I had taken a coaching approach to the situation instead of pushing someone to act when he did not see the need for action.

To approach it from a coaching perspective, I would need to shift from the boss trying to get my boss off my back to one of empathy when I look at the situation from the soldier's perspective.

116

He probably felt attacked. I threw two issues at him that he did not consider to be issues. He was tired of hearing about the card. Why should he invest energy in fixing a problem that the Army should not have caused in the first place? Why should he let the Army interfere in his personal life? Hadn't he given the Army enough of his time?

What would it have looked like in a coaching framework?

Coaching can take on a lot of different looks. There are so many different coaches out there: executive coaches, leadership development coaches, career coaches, business coaches, life coaches, and the list goes on. Some coaches are internal to the organization. Other coaches are hired from outside the organization. Some coaches focus on individuals. Some coaches work with teams. There are a lot of different ways to approach coaching. We're going to look at it from the internal coach perspective. We will take a look at the differences between individual coaching and team coaching, but first, we need to know where to start.

There are a few elements that can be applied to a successful coaching engagement.

- Trust and Rapport
- Safety
- Goal Setting
- Feedback and Learning
- Development and Growth

Trust and rapport create the foundation that allows coaching to take place. Your followers cannot open up and share with you if they cannot trust you and cannot speak with you. Trust is so important to building relationships. Trust comes from transparent communication, honesty, and words and actions that match. The more personal leadership styles focus on building relationships and emphasize communication. Rapport is the ability of people to connect with each other. Rapport comes from

117

the belief that it is safe for the other person to talk. Most people have had leaders who appeared to be unapproachable because of their personality or position. Other leaders create an environment that feels safe for people to approach them. The same elements that build trust, transparent communication, honesty, and words and actions that match can set conditions for building rapport. People feel more comfortable opening up when they can trust the person. Empathy and emotional intelligence skills will go a long way in relationship building. Vulnerability is another way to build trust and rapport. When a leader is willing to open up and share about themselves, it creates an environment where people can talk freely. It is not always easy to share, but the more you can share, the more your followers can share.

Safety is an interesting concept in coaching. Safety can be created by having a safe place to have a conversation. Safety can be knowing that what is said won't be judged. People have a guard that they keep up to protect themselves. Getting people to open up and lower their guard requires an element of safety. If you are a leader on a construction site, you may want to have a conversation in the truck to prevent people from hearing the conversation or walking into the job trailer. If you are a leader in a factory, you may want to go into a conference room with a door. If you're a leader in an office, you may want to have the conversation in a closed office instead of the cubicle area. The choice of location will impact the scope of the discussion. Empathy is also important to safety. Validation and not judging can create safety for your followers. When you validate your follower, you are giving credibility to their feelings. You are allowing them to have authority in their experience. When you hold back judgment, you are allowing the follower to work through a vulnerable area without negativity. Judgment will shut down the process for the follower. They will default to a subject that provides acceptance.

Goal setting is a key element of coaching. When we look at coaching in terms of sports, the goal is winning games. When we look at goal setting in our context, it is setting personal and professional goals. The goals should be SMART: specific, measurable, achievable, relevant, and time-bound.

- Specific – Make sure the goal is not too broad; if it is, set multiple goals to achieve the broad goal.
- Measurable – Frame the goal where it can be measured.
- Achievable – The goal needs to be reachable with the resources the person has access to.
- Relevant – The goal should fit into the work or personal life of the person.
- Time-bound – The goal shouldn't be to someday achieve; it should have a goal date.

Feedback and learning close the loop for the follower. This is the area where coaching teaches skills to handle situations when the leader can't give direction. During feedback, the leader shares observations about the follower's performance and progress on goals. The feedback should be a conversation with input from both sides. The follower should talk about their perspective on progress as well as the leader's perspective. The leader can then share information or resources that develop learning. Learning is an area of coaching that has the most variation. Some coaches focus on listening and talking through problems. Other coaches like to spend a lot of time on learning and teaching skills. The right amount of skill development with the follower will depend on you and your follower. There is not the right amount of skill development.

Development and growth are what coaching is all about. The follower should see growth out of the coaching relationship. Growth should be tied to the goals that are set but should not be limited to those areas. With a development and growth focus, leaders can look for positive change with followers. One area leaders should look for growth is in the confidence of followers to make decisions. The coaching sessions should build the follower's confidence to make decisions that they know align with their own growth and your position. The relationship is what builds the confidence. The follower learns more about the leader in the engagement.

I want to go back to when I didn't coach SGT L.

I did not have the best relationship with that specific Soldier, but I did practice transparent communication with my Soldiers. My soldiers could always speak freely with me. I don't think I would have had the strongest foundation for coaching, but I think it was a good starting point.

While I held the discussion in my office with the door shut, I could have found a better spot for the discussion. We didn't have a ceiling, and it was not the most private environment. It had a semi-private feel. Think of a warehouse with concrete floors, block walls, and small office spaces that were framed and drywalled but didn't extend the ceiling line. There was probably 7 feet of open space above the walls. If I wanted a coaching session, I could have potentially improved his feeling of safety by finding a different location.

I didn't work with him to set goals. I told him what to do, but there was no collaboration. There was no focus on why the actions were relevant. If I wanted to coach, I could have worked with him to develop goals that satisfied the actions I wanted him to complete.

SGT L was a leader. I could have used a coaching session to develop his skills by teaching him why it mattered. I could have helped him develop his own why. There was a broken process that he could help future Soldiers with, but instead, it was a directive process that did not add to his skillset. There was also a gap in the feedback loop. It took me a month to find out he never made any action after the first conversation. Following up could have brought the conversation to a coaching conversation.

Lastly, I wasn't worried about his development or growth. I wanted my leadership off my back. If I had been deliberate, he could have taken something away from the experience that helped him develop as a leader. To make it a coaching session, education and follow-up would be needed.

At the time, I didn't have coaching as a tool in my toolbox. Now that I have it in my toolbox, I can use it formally and informally with my followers.

Coaching allows me to meet with my team members and find out where they are and where they want to go.

You can use coaching to connect with your team. It may not feel natural at first. There may be elements that feel scripted, but the longer you practice, the more natural it will feel. The first step may be the most uncomfortable, but the most important is the next step, regardless of where you are.

INDIVIDUAL COACHING

Individual coaching is when the leader works with individual team members on a one-on-one basis. The leader has private conversations with team members and builds the relationship. Trust and rapport, safety, goal setting, feedback and learning, and development and growth targets are focused on each member of the team. The leader invests a significant amount of time into each of the team members.

One of the benefits of individual coaching is the confidentiality that is afforded to the team members. If you have two team members who do not get along with each other, they do not have to air their dirty laundry in front of each other. They have the space to have the conversation individually with their leader. The leader can help both team members navigate the issue without having to share the other team member's feedback. The leader develops the team by providing one-on-one feedback that is not shared outside of the relationship. Confidentiality is essential to maintaining safety in the relationship.

One-on-one coaching opens a power-dynamic consideration for the leader and the team member. The leader usually holds a position of power that can affect coaching sessions. Team members do not want to say the wrong thing and experience punishment or judgment from someone in a position of authority. Leaders must find a way to remove or reduce power dynamic issues that prevent team members from sharing. Leaders who can express vulnerability have an easier time reducing the power consideration. The team members need to know that it is safe to share. The leader needs to be able to maintain their authority outside of the coaching session. The balance will take practice but will stabilize with time.

The focus of individual coaching is the personal and professional development goals, aspirations, and challenges of the team members. The leader serving as a coach works with each team member to develop the skills and self-awareness to achieve their desired results. The individual focus of individual coaching allows the leader to work with each individual at different stages of their progression. The leader may find one team member who is prone to conflict with their teammates. The leader can coach the individual through emotional intelligence and empathy techniques to help reduce conflict. At the same time, the leader can pass on task-specific skills to help prepare an employee for a promotion. The focus follows the needs of each individual.

Goals are defined by the leader and the team members. The goals may nest with the larger focus of the team, or they may focus on personal growth. I have had Soldiers who did not plan to stay in the Army. The goals that I set with those Soldiers are different than the goals that I set with Soldiers who plan to do a second enlistment or a career. By defining goals that suit the individual, you create a bond that improves performance regardless of their long-term goals.

Outcomes are seen across the board. Each individual who is coached will have different outcomes. Some of the outcomes will be stronger individual contributor outcomes, while others will have better social outcomes that reduce conflict. With individual coaching, each relationship will have a different outcome. The name says it. When we coach on an individual basis, we are looking at the contributions that each team member can provide.

TEAM COACHING

Team coaching is more comparable to the sports analogy. When we look at team coaching, we are looking at how the team functions together. The relationship between the leader and the team will play into how the team receives the coaching.

In team coaching, the coach is looking for opportunities to reduce friction points, increase efficiency, and reduce the cycle cost for whatever is being produced. On a new construction site, the leader may act as a coach by helping the team members identify areas to anticipate work so there is less time spent standing around waiting for direction. The leader may work to increase the communication that is taking place between team members so that it does not need to filter through the leader to make something happen. The team may proactively identify where materials will be needed so that work does not wait for materials to be transported when it could take place at the same time as another task.

Confidentiality has less of a role in team coaching. Team coaching looks to share information across the team. What is said is intended for a broader audience. Leaders would do well to praise in public and correct in private when it comes to individual contributors. Maintain confidentiality if an individual has an area to improve, but be sure to offer praise publicly. Team members will appreciate corrections on a one-to-one basis that does not make them feel embarrassed.

The power dynamic for team coaching will depend on the relationship you have developed with the team and their perception of power distance. Power distance is the level of autonomy team members feel in working with their leader. Low power distance allows the team to speak up and share their concerns. High power distance will limit how often the team speaks up to share their concerns. Understanding how your team perceives your position and the power that it holds will help you shape the way you coach the team.

Team coaching focuses on the interconnections between the different team members. Do the team members know when they need to pick up the ball and make forward movement, or do they need to pass the ball to someone who is in a better position? All of the parts make a whole, and the leader needs to look at each team member's contributions to understand when and where opportunities for improvement are.

Goals are geared towards the overall capabilities of the team. The leader should work with team input to define SMART goals. The goal may be quota or quality-based but will reflect team performance and not individual contributors.

Outcomes are geared towards communication, collaboration, and conflict resolution. A team that works in synch with each other produces more results at a higher quality than a team who does not know how to work together. Clear communication helps to reduce confusion and increase purpose on the job site. Collaboration uses input from across the team to develop a solution rather than a single perspective. Conflict resolution reduces the time spent off task dealing with personality differences. People generally have a similar purpose, but it can be lost in small differences.

COMMUNICATION

Everything starts with a thought. How we move that thought from the thinker to the next person is communication. The thought becomes a message that is sent. The message is then perceived by another person. The problem with communication is we have constant interference in our communication that changes the way that our messages are received.

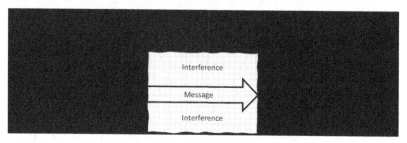

The initial thought and the final perception are hopefully close to what we are looking for, but sometimes, it is drastically different from what we intended. We can reduce the impact of interference by creating a feedback loop.

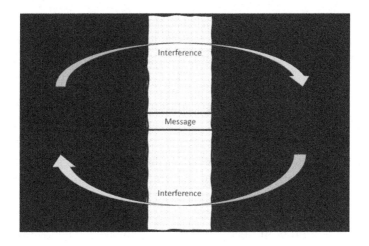

When the receiver shares the message that was understood back with the sender, the sender can refine the message and ensure clarity to move the target back to where it was intended. The back-and-forth process ensures that everyone understands the message. The feedback process looks different depending on the number of receivers and the way the message is being shared.

In developing our leadership toolbox, clear communication is essential. Communication can be a tool in itself, or it can allow us to use other tools within our toolbox more effectively.

Emotional intelligence starts with the recognition of thoughts about our reaction to a situation. We then progress to a point where we recognize how other people feel as a result of what is happening around them. The final step in emotional intelligence is relationship management. We manage relationships by offering clear communication that delivers the message in a way the receiver can connect with. Transparent communication helps to eliminate anxiety or discomfort that a team member may have. Transparent communication limits the fear that the sender is hiding bad news in their message. It is not always comfortable and may require tough conversations, but it ensures that people trust the communication. Clear communication also helps with relationship management because people understand what the communication is intended to convey. Clear communication is when the message sent and the message received most closely match the thought the sender had.

Empathy starts with communication from the receiver position. Leaders practicing empathy need to actively listen to their followers. Active listening is a process where the leader looks to reduce the interference in the communication process. The leader who is taking in the follower's communication is removing barriers to the communication process. The leader does this by using the SLANT method: sit up, lean forward, ask questions, nod your head, and track the speaker. The leader also needs to practice effective communication from the sender role. The leader needs to use language that validates rather than minimizes the follower's perspective. Not projecting or conveying judgment also requires deliberate use of language. The words we use can have a profound effect on the message the receiver hears. Having a teenager in my house, I often find that my choice of words has a different meaning than what she hears. I say something, and it has a different meaning for her.

Motivating followers begins with the way we communicate. In the discussion on Theory X versus Theory Y, we are communicating through words or deeds the level of starting motivation we think our team has. If we are micromanaging because we believe the team has a Theory X mentality, we are communicating that the team does not need to be independent thinkers. When we offer the team freedom to be creative because we think they have a Theory Y mentality, we are communicating that they have the freedom to try new things.

The way we communicate with our team also determines the level of needs we are looking to satisfy within the workplace. Talks of teamwork and support build-up at the love and belonging level of Maslow's hierarchy of needs. Praise and recognition are forms of communication that build self-esteem.

Communication that focuses on meeting full potential will raise the team's ability to reach self-actualization.

A person-centric focus in communication or a task focus in communication will tell the team about your engagement focus. A balanced approach will lead your followers to see you as a middle-of-the-road manager or a team manager. A high focus on people will lead your team to see you from a country club-style management perspective. Focusing only on tasks will lead the team to see you as an authority compliance manager. No communication about either will lead the team to see you as an impoverished manager. Where we place our focus on our communication impacts the way our followers see us.

One of the hardest lessons to learn in communication is that we are always communicating, regardless of whether we intend to or not. A lack of communication sends a message. Communication is wrapped into our posture and body language. Our body language can override the message that we are saying with our words. Effective communication begins with ensuring that all of the messages we are sending tell the same story.

We also need to remember that once a message gets out, it is hard to undo the message. The impact of negative communication can cause followers to leave an organization. Communication can build or spend leadership capital. Deliberate communication builds leadership capital, whereas unintentional communication can deplete leadership capital quickly. Unintentional or off-the-cuff communication is often intended to convey a minor thought, but it will be pulled through the lens of others who may have a different perspective.

While I was in the Army, I had a role where we did the same training every few months. The training was very predictable with the events that needed to be completed. It is important to note there were other companies doing the same training, but the cycles were staggered. One of the higher unit commanders would visit the training sessions and give directions to execute the training differently in the next cycle. We would execute in his direction the next cycle, but he would get upset and tell us to do it the way we had performed in the previous cycle. He was upset because he had forgotten who and when he had communicated with. He had given similar advice to the other companies who had executed the variation earlier, and he did not like it. Because he didn't know who he had told to do it which way, he was often frustrated by the results. We were often frustrated because we received inconsistent communication. The breakdown was communication. The break in communication often left us questioning whether or not we should implement the change.

Communication tore away at that commander's credibility with his junior leaders. The team did not know whether the communication was an off-the-cuff remark or a deliberate communication.

Understanding who we are communicating with and how we are communicating with them can increase our effectiveness as leaders.

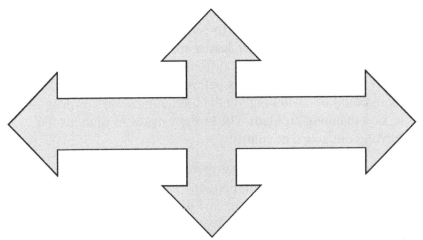

Communication needs to flow in all directions. Leaders often think about how they communicate within the team or with followers, down. Unless the leader is at the top of the organization, with no board or shareholders, there is always someone above who needs communication. The leader typically has peers within the organization who would benefit from communication sideways. As leaders, we need to lead up and across as much as we are leading down.

When we communicate up the chain, we help manage our leaders' expectations. It is easy to limit communications upwards to only when there is a request or a need. Proactively communicating upwards has benefits.

- Early problem identification
- Resource reallocation
- Trust
- Continuous flow of work

When we share how things are going with our leadership, we give them the opportunity to help **identify potential problems** before they become problems. Our leaders want us to be successful. Our success drives their success. An advantage that our leaders typically have is the ability to view a breadth of the organization that we don't get to see. If we identify what we think is a small problem, our leader may have seen a similar problem go off the rails with a different team. Communicating upwards allows them to help us before the problem grows. The problem could be switching vendors, an engineering or design issue, or a manning problem. The leader can see resolutions that are beyond our scope of control.

Resource reallocation is a way that our leaders can help us with problems. If you've ever thought, "I need to figure out what to do with these team members for two weeks," because you didn't have the volume of work, you tried to handle a problem at your level that could have been solved easily by the next level up. You may have a peer who is thinking, "I'm going to have to have my team work overtime to meet this deadline" because there are not enough resources on that site. Communicating upwards allows your job to increase or decrease resources if there is another place to put them. Your scope may not allow you to reallocate resources on your own, but your boss may be able to help you out.

Bad news does not get better with time. Your leaders will **trust** you more if they know what is going on. Waiting until the problem has grown beyond control will reduce the chances that your boss can help you. Your leadership cannot get you additional resources if they do not know there is a problem that needs support. Your leadership will be likely to see someone they cannot trust who hides problems, as opposed to the leader who gets things done. When you highlight a problem and bring a solution, it builds trust. You are proactive in the process.

Your leaders will also ensure that your team has a **continuous flow of work** if you are communicating upwards.

Leaders assign work where there is capacity and trust. When you communicate with your leadership, they know when you are at, above, or below capacity. Communication helps keep that flow continuous. Your leadership will also know that your team can be trusted to get the job done. Transparency in communication helps to identify the strengths and weaknesses of your team. Your leadership can choose to play to your team's strengths or give you opportunities to improve weaknesses and become a stronger team.

I had a miserable role as a program manager. We had a lot of issues. My immediate leadership was aware of the issues because I was communicating upwards. The problem was that the executive leadership needed to be informed because the program had the potential to lose a lot of money and/or destroy a relationship with a strategic customer. My leaders did not have the resources necessary to get us back on track. The problems began to escalate until they could no longer be contained. Two layers of leadership above me were fired over the way they dealt with the program. The executive leadership was not able to identify any of the problems or reallocate resources. Trust was broken to the point where two levels of leadership were dismissed. In the end, the program team did not get any follow-on work and were laid off. The bottleneck in upward communication is one of the leading causes of program failure.

It is easier to tell stories where upwards communication failed, and there was a disaster than stories where it was successful. The reason is that where it is successful, it often leads to gradual increases for everyone. There is less of a climax to the successful stories. Leaders recognize how they can help, and they do. Everyone stays happy.

When communicating down, I find it helpful to identify how the work being completed fits into the larger picture. Lower levels of leadership in the organization often lack insight into why changes are being made or why they need to take on a project that doesn't look attractive. Understanding the impact and importance helps the team rally around the cause.

When communicating with your team, ask yourself what they would need to know to complete the task if you weren't there. There is always the potential for tragedy, leaving the team short of a leader, but there is also the potential for the leader to be selected for a promotion. The team needs the 5 Ws.

- **Who** is the work being done for?
- **What** is the work to be completed?
- **Where** does the work need to be done?
- **When** is the deadline?
- **Why** is this an important project?

The team should know their role on the team. Understanding the scope of the work is vital for accomplishing the task.

I jumped into the program manager role right after the project kicked off. I communicated with my team that our first priority was the quality of work. I was willing to accept a higher cost to ensure that we were successful in the first set of sites. My leadership was willing to assume risk on initial costs if it secured the customer's relationship. Our second priority was the timeliness of the work. The work needed to be completed on time. The cost was our third priority. There are three variables that can be leveraged.

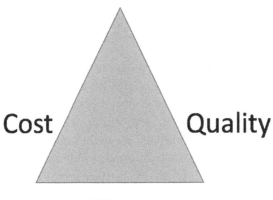

Cost   Quality

Time

In my program, the intention was to start reducing costs after the program was fully established. Quality would be maintained through repetition, and time would be reduced through experience. The team had to understand where the priorities were. I could not be the only one who understood the priority. The reason behind the priorities was just as important. The team needed to know why we were prioritizing the way we were in order for everyone to be on the same page.

When communicating with your team, the more information you can share, the greater chance they have of success. Transparent communication builds trust. You may need to be mindful of their interests and time. Not everyone is interested in all of the details. Work with your team to understand the level of detail they are looking for. Fill in all the pertinent details without overwhelming them with information that does not pertain to them. It will take balance, but the right level of information will empower your team to act.

Communicating sideways expands your view of the organization and builds support for when you need help. Whether your peers are leading teams similar to yours or they are leading teams with completely different functions, you will benefit from knowing what is going on in their world and sharing what is going on in your world.

In the Army, we talked about adjacent units in our area. We needed to know whose space we could potentially end up in or who could end up in our space. We each brought different capabilities with us. When we build relationships and communicate with those around us, we get a better view of what is taking place in our larger environment. We can pick up tips and tricks for dealing with problems as they arise. We also have the opportunity to provide support to each other without worrying about our leadership reassigning resources.

While it is great for a leader to reassign resources, if I have a peer who has additional resources I could use, I can cut down on the time required to get the support. It also provides me the opportunity to provide the same support.

There is no right or wrong way to build communication sideways. The key is starting the conversation. What you can learn will pay for the time you spend focusing on someone else's area. You will learn more about the business by hearing about your peers.

When I was a general manager, I found talking to my peers to be one of the most helpful times that I had. I was able to hear how they had already dealt with similar personnel problems to what I was encountering and learn how the company had grown to its current position. There were lots of little tidbits of information that made me more successful because I had advice from others. We were able to keep crews working because they could travel between different markets.

Push, Pull, and Pooled

When is it time to send communication?

Communication can be pushed. There is no request for communication, but the information owner sends it anyway.

Communication can be pulled. Someone needs information, sends a request, and then the information owner pulls it together and sends it out.

Communication can be pooled. A lot of organizations have databases that allow users to pull reports. Pooled information is information that is put into the database whenever it is needed.

There is a time and a place for each type of communication.

Push communication is great for proactively sending messages before there is a request. When we push communication up our leadership chain, we are giving our leaders a chance to help identify issues before they become issues.

In the Army, we used the term SITREP or situation report. The purpose of a SITREP is to provide an update on what a unit is doing. The report is often brief and may or may not have a formulaic approach, depending on where you are. The value of the SITREP is the unit commander knew what was going on in the field. The SITREP could be prepared in advance and sent at a time that was convenient for the reporting unit.

One of the key elements of push communication is that it is sent prior to a request for information being submitted. The information is proactive. The proactive nature means I can prepare it when I have time in my schedule. I do not have to drop everything I am doing to gather the necessary information.

An advantage of push communication is that it makes you look like you have solid control of the situation. When you push information, you are anticipating needs and answering questions before they arise. Most leaders will not dig too deep into push communication. They may ask a few follow-up questions, but they will not be digging for information that you have not already referenced. Push communication establishes control over the information flow and allows you to provide updates at the right moment for you.

Pull communication is the opposite of push communication. Your leadership is asking for information that you have not prepared and are not ready to send. Pull communication usually comes with a timeline for a response. You are now pulling together information in a format specified by someone else and due when you may have other commitments. The downside to pulling communication is that you will need to drop what you are doing to make time to answer the mail on the communication request.

Requests for communication are an opportunity to learn what information your leadership is looking for. When you receive a pull request, look into what is driving the request for information.

If the information request is a one-off, it is unlikely that you would have been prepared to answer the question proactively. If the request came once, it may come again. Take note of where you pulled the information from and look for opportunities to streamline the data pull in the future. The information may be worth tracking for you moving forward.

If the information is a recurring requirement, it is important to understand whether it is a new requirement or an existing requirement. Suppose the request for information is a new requirement. In that case, it is an indication that the organization is looking to expand its level of understanding at the execution level. This could be a refinement of processes, which is a positive. It could also be to place tighter controls around the execution level of the organization to prevent losses.

If the information request is an existing recurring requirement that you have not been meeting, this is a great opportunity to reach up and sideways. Make sure you answer the requirements, but ask your leaders and your peers about information requirements. Often, leaders think people know things that they have never been told. This is an opportunity to learn if there are other requirements that you were unaware of.

When I was a platoon leader and a company commander, I often thought I was in a good place with what I was tracking. I would later get a pull communication request that informed me just how wrong I was. I learned a lot about what mattered to my leaders by not being able to answer questions on the spot. Something my leaders considered valuable that I was not tracking closely became a drill to get the information in time. I learned to track information based on the pull communication requests I received.

Pooled communication is the information we report that goes into a database. A lot of organizations have electronic or paper systems for reporting information to the organization's headquarters. The information, at a minimum, consists of information to pay employees and bill customers. Some organizations ask for information to track fleet equipment usage. Other organizations will ask for information about site conditions, weather, material status, or safety questions.

I've been in organizations where the field resisted inputting pooled communication. They would turn in enough information to close out the form, but they did not always provide accurate information. Marking a 1 in a quantity field so it had data and moving on. The lack of effort was often because the field did not see value in providing accurate and timely data. They made sure employees could be paid, and they moved on.

Accurate pooled communication eliminates the need for pulling communication in many situations. An increased requirement for pooled communication is not intended to place an additional burden on the field but to increase the value of the data collected. The information can be used to more accurately estimate jobs, which creates tighter margin control. The information can be used to hone in on high-performing crews to learn from what they are doing.

Providing the requested communication can benefit your team. As a leader, you are providing safety for your team. When the company has more consistent margins, it can manage raises and bonuses more effectively. They do not have to hold off because they don't know how some of the jobs will perform.

Pooled communication can be a resource for you as a leader. Explore the data and the reporting to look for information you can report back to your team. Productivity is a common metric you can pull from pooled communication. The data allows you to push information down to your team. When we work for companies, we need to demonstrate the value that we bring. Productivity is a real metric that establishes how well we are doing as a team. You can use communication to make sure the team knows how the team is performing.

Regardless of the way information is requested, the faster and more confidently you can deliver the message, the more trust you will build with your leadership and your team.

When we send a message, it communicates our confidence with the message. The longer we hold on to information, the less time the receiver will have with the message before it becomes outdated.

Learn from the information that is requested and that you share. You should be able to learn what matters to your team and organization as you communicate. Knowing what and when to communicate will help you understand what matters to each group that you work with.

FACE-TO-FACE, PHONE, EMAIL, AND CARRIER PIGEON

Up, down, and sideways gave us an opportunity to look at who we should be communicating with. Push, pull, and pool helped us identify when we should be communicating. This section looks at the way we communicate.

The environment we live and work in offers us an astounding number of ways to communicate. I can talk to someone in person. I can use video chat software like Zoom, Webex, or Teams. I can call someone on the phone. I can email a short or lengthy message. I can send a text message. I have the ability to post flyers and hope that the right person sees the message on the flyer. I can post on social media and hope that the right person sees the message. You can write a book and hope that someone picks it off the shelf. The only form of sending the message I don't think I can use effectively is a carrier pigeon. I am pretty sure that they need to be raised where the message is returned. I also don't know my confidence level in pulling the message off the bird's leg.

With the vast number of ways we can communicate with each other, we need to evaluate the upsides and the downsides of each communication type. Consider the tone your message has when you send it through different channels. Think about the speed at which you can get a message across. How much detail does your message need to be sent to the receivers? Do you need to communicate with a group of people? Does your message need to go through multiple layers of the organization?

Our choices of communication methods affect the way that our message is received. Two people can read a message and interpret the message differently. One person may find a rude message that is dripping with sarcasm, while the other person reads a message that is direct and to the point. Interference has many shapes and forms.

141

Interference can be caused by internal factors that reside within the receiver, external factors around the communication, and factors that connect the receiver and the sender. Understanding the cause of interference allows you to improve communication. Whether you are the sender working to remove interference in your communication or you are the receiver working to limit the interference in the communication you are receiving. Common sources of interference are:

- Cultural Differences
- Jargon and Technical Terms
- Internal Bias
- Emotions and Stress
- Nature of the Relationship
- Power Dynamic
- Information Overload
- Environmental Noise
- Visual Distractions
- Technology Issues
- Physical Distance

There are a lot of potential causes for interference. The way we speak and the way we choose to communicate will impact the overall perception of the message we are sending.

People pay attention to more than one sense at any given point in time. When you are communicating with people, be aware of how many senses your message will occupy. We typically focus on engaging with words and imagery when we think of communication. If I am speaking with someone in a personal manner, I may put my hand on their shoulder, pat their arm, or just shake their hand at the start of a conversation. I worked with a human resource director who believed in sharing meals with people prior to making a hiring decision. He always spoke of it as breaking bread. The communication that is shared at a table brings in a new set of senses to the communication.

You have the smells and tastes of the food and drinks. You have the background noise that influences how conversation is heard. When you are looking at a meal as a background for a conversation, that meal can influence how the message is received. People who are picky eaters may become too focused on a distaste for what is around them. Foodies may become too focused on what is around them to hear the message. I agree with communicating while breaking bread, but it is important to ensure that the location supports the message.

With as many factors as there are to consider in reducing interference, is there a best form of communication?

No.

There are some great forms of communication for each situation, though.

Face-to-face communication is typically considered one of the best forms of communication. You are able to effectively communicate with at least two senses. Face-to-face communication will, at a minimum, hit the auditory and visual senses. You can hear and see the person you are speaking with. The communication allows the sender and receiver to ask questions in real-time without delay. The visual component allows both the sender and the receiver to read the body language of the other person. Both people can see whether or not the other person is engaged in the communication.

A fun fact about body language: when two people are talking to each other, the direction of each person's feet is an indicator of whether they want to be part of the conversation. When the feet are facing the other person, the person is engaged in the conversation. When the feet are pointed away, the person has the ability to step away from the conversation with fewer obstructions, and they are less engaged. Most elements of body language are naturally decoded, but some require explaining.

When engaging in face-to-face communication, be aware of the messages you are sending non-verbally as well as verbally. If you are speaking to a group and utilizing graphics, be aware of whether or not the graphics add to what you are saying or detract from the message you want to send. Too much information on a screen can eliminate the receivers' attention from what you are saying. Practice empathy when you are engaging in face-to-face communication. Active listening will help you engage and develop a perspective that includes the other person's perspective.

One downside to face-to-face communication is the lack of a recording. People can walk away from the communication and forget what was said or have a different interpretation of the events. It is always helpful to follow face-to-face communication with written communication if possible.

Phone communication can serve as a backup to face-to-face communication, but it only engages the auditory sense and can be prone to technical issues. Phone calls are great for answering quick questions that do not need to be scheduled. The phone can interrupt someone's workflow, and they have the ability to decide to answer the phone or let it go to voicemail and return the call at a more convenient time.

For a long time, phone communication was second to face-to-face communication in real-time communication. Phones allow us to bridge distances without the need to travel to a central location. Even on a job site, it may not be convenient to drop a task and meet in a central location. Phone communication allows both parties to operate from where they are already located.

A downside to phone communication is the lack of visual sense, which reduces accountability during a conversation and encourages multi-tasking. Either party is likely to work on something else and not give the communication the attention that is required during the conversation. I had a project manager who worked for me who told me that I could never multi-task. You can serial-task. You shift your focus back and forth between multiple work streams. You do not successfully focus on multiple work streams at the same time. Whatever is taking place during the phone conversation may have reduced attention, while the phone call also gets reduced attention. While it is important to be aware of the potential, it is not a reason to abandon the method.

A second downside to phone communication is the lack of a recording. Just like face-to-face communication, people can walk away from the communication and forget what was said or have a different interpretation of the events. Follow up with written communication if possible.

Video Conferencing Software is up with face-to-face communication depending on the organizational norms. Video conferencing has the ability to engage both the auditory and visual senses. The software also allows people to share their desktops and present information without the need to bring everyone to a central location. When work is geographically separated, video conference software closes the distance and brings people to a central virtual location.

Not all organizations use the camera functionality of video conference software. Many team members keep their cameras off. There is a sense of inviting people into our private spaces when we turn on our cameras. Some people want to keep their privacy, while others look for the full engagement that is available with the camera on.

When we turn cameras on in a video conferencing software, we open the door to reading context. When people are geographically separated, there are likely to be accent differences that may make it harder to read if something is a joke or serious. People often don't have the opportunity to spend time in person getting to know each other before operating in a virtual environment where the person on the other end of the computer is a picture they've never met in person.

The software typically has recording and transcribing features that can be used to capture what took place during the call. Not everyone is comfortable with these features outside of training events. Use them with caution, but they do have the ability to capture the discussions that took place. It never hurts to send out a summary in written form of what was discussed.

Email is a blessing and a curse to the workforce. Email engages the visual sense but uses language processing. When we read emails, it can be extremely difficult to decipher whether someone is making a joke or being serious. If you do not know the sender well, it is best to assume that the sender means exactly what is written. I typically give the benefit of the doubt that the person on the other end of the email has good intentions, but it can be difficult to decipher.

One of the big upsides to emails is they are written directions that can be referred to as a way of capturing the task to be completed. You have to write what the expectations are.

Email is often overused within organizations. Everything becomes an email, and people spend more time sorting emails and looking for what pertains to them rather than doing the tasks they have been assigned.

Emails are great follow-ups for the first three methods of communication we have discussed so far.

One notable aspect of email is it is not real-time communication. Emails are sent when the sender thinks about the message, received when the receiver is available, and actioned when the receiver has capacity. There are ways to have a read receipt, but you will not always know when your message has been read if the receiver does not send a response/

Text messages and chats are another form of written communication but are less formal than email. Text messages

146

and chats can be real-time communication, but only if the other person is actively available to speak. The communication is often secondary to another task the person is working on at the same time.

The communication is often shorter and requires more back and forth than an email would. Both people need the ability to answer if clarification is needed. Text and chats are often point-to-point, including only two people, but they can also be group messages that allow multiple people to provide input.

The informality of the messages allows people to send messages faster but has the potential for misinterpretation, the same way emails can be misinterpreted. People may be more casual in messaging, leading to misinterpretations of jokes, humor, or context.

Like emails, messaging engages the visual sense and language processing. As it is written, it can serve as a record of what was needed, but it is often more difficult to retrieve than emails.

It's a great form of communication, but it has limitations as well. Some messaging platforms utilize other networking features that allow for collaboration on documents.

One-way communication is our use of flyers, emails sent from unmonitored email boxes, social media posts, and writing a book. One-way communication addresses a wide audience without confirming receipt from anyone. All of the different methods of one-way communication raise awareness of an idea, issue, or situation, but they do not capture everyone's attention. All of the methods require that people have their heads up when passing the message and that they will stop to read and engage in the message.

The communication is one-way because it does not spark dialogue with the creator. It may generate discussion in an open forum, but it has the same limitation: only people who see the message can engage with the message. While the creator may participate in the conversation if they are monitoring responses, that is often not the intent of the content.

One-way communication is intended to put information out to a wide audience. The information may be intended to provide support, or it may be intended to inform a future decision. As a leader, use the one-way communications you receive to drive conversations within your teams. When you see the information, follow up with your team to see if they have seen it. Drive conversations based on the information that you have seen.

As a leader, you are looking for opportunities to improve. One-way communication requires people to notice the message. When you see the message, ensure that you pass it along so you make it more active. These are opportunities for you to improve your team.

There are a number of ways you can engage in communication with people. It is important to ensure that you use the right communication method for the right communication message and audience.

When I reflect on my time in the Army Reserves, and my company was about to have our orders extended, I chose face-to-face communication with the company. I had to deliver a message that required emotional intelligence, empathy, and a way to build motivation. I could have talked to just a few of my leaders and had them spread the message. I could have put a flyer up on the operations tent to let people know. I could have sent information out over the radio. There were a lot of ways I could have communicated the message, but face-to-face in a horseshoe is the way I chose to share the message. I felt that the message was better served by real-time communication that allowed everyone an opportunity to ask questions and share their perspective on the news.

The way we communicate our messages sends our own messages. Our choice of communication style is often driven by the leadership style that we align with. People will make judgments on our leadership style based on the way that we communicate. When you are looking for your opportunity to communicate, be aware of how people will receive it. Think about the way it will reduce interference in the message that you are sending.

ORGANIZING YOUR TOOLBOX

As a leader, take time to reflect on who you want to be as a leader and who you are leading. Evaluate what you want to achieve as a leader. Decide where your leadership begins and ends. Do you know when you became a leader? Have you decided why you are in a leadership role?

In developing your leadership toolbox, understanding the 5 Ws of leadership will allow you to be informed about the type of leader you want to be. Leadership has a lot of definitions and often has different meanings from person to person. There is an academic line between leader and manager, but functionally, there is a road that you will need to walk to find a balance that meets your organization's needs and the needs of your team.

The toolbox is only a metaphor for the skills that we can use, but I believe it is an apt metaphor. When I think about my toolbox, I have a handful of hammers that have different purposes. Each hammer is intended for a specific set of functions. I get frustrated when my wife grabs a roofing hammer out of my toolbox to put up a picture hook. It's not the right tool. It may get the job done, but if not used correctly, it has the potential to cause damage that I will need to come back and fix. When you think of leadership, think of the skills you have as tools that can support you in the situations that you find yourself in.

The first four tools we discussed are emotional intelligence, empathy, motivation, and engagement. Those tools will help you in just about any situation. Like my wife with the roofing hammer, it is the right type of tool for most situations, even if it is not the only solution. Those four tools allow for the human connection between you and your team. Focus on emotional intelligence and empathy, to begin with. Both tools are interconnected and create a framework where you can be successful in leading.

When you are comfortable with emotional intelligence and empathy, start evaluating the motivation of your team members.

Are all your team members the same in their needs? Do some team members have different motivations than others? Probe your evaluation of where their needs are being met. Do not be afraid to ask their input on what drives them. Asking questions does not mean that you are a bad boss; it means that you care.

Once you begin to develop an understanding of where your team is, look at how you engage the team. This part can be uncomfortable. Self-evaluation is often uncomfortable. We are either overly critical of ourselves because we are focused on the negative, or we only sing our own praises so that we feel good about ourselves. This is another area where it makes sense to bring your team into the discussion. Ask your team where they see you as a leader. Do they see you as task-focused? Do they see you as people-focused? Is there where you want to be?

When you have the first four foundational tools under your belt, you can begin to shape the way you use the tools. You can begin to put shape to the style of leader you want to be.

Many leaders adopt multiple leadership styles to fit the situation they find themselves in. Different team members may focus on different traits of the leader's style and come up with a different perspective. That is fine. The larger question is, are you happy with the way you are leading your team? Are you effectively leading your team?

If the answer is no to either question, it is time to try a new leadership style.

Leadership should be like a fingerprint. Each of us has our own style that leaves a unique imprint on those that we touch.

As you develop your leadership style, I encourage you to incorporate coaching as an element of your style. Use coaching to build your team and strengthen those around you. Coaching

151

is a tool by itself. Coaching will be supported by having the four foundational tools, but it is a great tool to build your team.

Lastly, find a communication strategy that works for you. There are a lot of elements to manage in communication, but the more we practice. The better we get. Communication is woven through every tool we have discussed. It is a part of the tools, but it is also a tool that stands on its own.

Reflection Questions

1. How would you define leadership after reading the book?
2. What tool do you think is the easiest to learn?
3. What tool do you think is the hardest to learn?
4. Do you have an idea about the kind of leader you want to be?
5. Do you have an idea about the kind of leader you don't want to be?
6. Do you have anyone coaching you?
7. Are you able to coach your team?
8. Are you communicating in all the directions you should be?
9. Do you know when and how to get communication to the right people?
10. How do you want to deliver your messages?

If you are new to leadership, I hope you find it as fulfilling as I do. If you are experienced in leadership, I hope you find joy in leading that you can pass on.

Made in the USA
Middletown, DE
05 February 2024